CATCH TENCH

THE ANGLING TIMES LIBRARY

CATCH
TENCH

WITH

JOHN WILSON

B🌿XTREE

in association with
ANGLING TIMES

First published in Great Britain in 1991 by Boxtree Limited
This paperback edition first published in 1994

Text and photographs © John Wilson 1991
Illustrations © Boxtree Limited 1991

3 5 7 9 10 8 6 4 2

Angling Times is a weekly newspaper produced by EMAP
Publishing Limited, Bretton, Peterborough. Established
in 1953, it is Britain's biggest selling weekly fishing
publication.

Illustrations by David Batten
Cover designed by Geoff Hayes
Colour origination by Fotographics, Hong Kong
Printed and bound in the UK by Cambus Litho Ltd for

Boxtree Limited
Broadwall House
21 Broadwall
London SE1 9PL

A CIP catalogue entry for this book is available from the
British Library.

ISBN 0 7522 1009 2

CONTENTS

ACKNOWLEDGEMENTS

No angling writer can produce a book without considerable help from others. Allow me therefore to thank the editing and design team, the mates who leave their own fishing to photograph me, and a very special thank you to good friend Dave Batten who has made such a fine job of the line drawings.

John Wilson
Great Witchingham
1991

INTRODUCTION

A S I sincerely trust the reader will discover within the following pages, there is a surfeit of interesting, challenging and exciting methods of catching tench. Space has prevented me from providing details of every conceivable technique: indeed, would it not be rather presumptuous even to suggest that I know them all. For I am sure I do not. That is the everlasting strength and wonder of our sport. No one ever knows it all and we never stop learning from each other, from the environment in which we live and fish, and of course from the fish themselves.

This book is therefore a collection of my experiences and thoughts on tench fishing covering a wide spectrum of still waters and rivers, paying great detail in so far as location is concerned to the kinds of habitat in which tench prefer to live. After all, I know of no better way of contacting another person than by knocking on their front door. And to be successful at catching tench, whatever its size, this invariably proves the most rewarding approach.

I have purposefully avoided the trap of advising you on how best to catch specimen tench because this is a book of techniques which, once practised, open the door to catching tench of all sizes, wherever you fish.

Besides, exactly at what size does a tench become a specimen? Is it the traditional yardstick of 5 lb (which I still hold sacred), or fish of 7, 8 and 9 lb which nowadays are being regularly taken from selected southern fisheries, particularly rich reservoirs and mature gravel pits.

I rather imagine the angler with limited local prospects of overstocked ponds and small pits where tench average between 2 and 3 lb would be overjoyed at capturing a 4-pounder. And the northerner with only the local canal to fish would indeed be happy with a tench of half that weight.

So please learn to appreciate the species as a creature and each technique as just one route among many towards its capture. Techniques you can vary, adjust and enjoy experimenting with throughout an entire lifetime – come on, come and catch some tench with me.

CHAPTER ONE

THE SPECIES

TENCH
(*Tinca tinca*)

With its distinctive olive green livery, tiny red 'teddy bear eyes' and dark grey-brown fins, the tench is seldom confused, by fishermen, with any other species. Even those who never practise the gentle art will know of the tench by its odd name and be aware of its green body, for there is not another freshwater species so unusually coloured. Yet we take its unique friendly form for granted.

Even with the escalating popularity of carp during the past few years, the tench remains a firm summer favourite amongst UK anglers and their counterparts in most European countries, although European anglers unfortunately are not so keen on returning tench of an edible size. Its delicate, sweet, white flesh is highly prized right across the continent, and in Asia where tench are intensively farmed for food.

A phenomenon surrounding the tench and no other species, something which has been handed down over the years from one angling writer to another, is its nickname of 'doctor fish'. It used to be thought that a tench only needs to rub up against a fish of another species ailing from open wounds, and it's on the mend. Well, maybe its thick coating of slime does contain some kind of medicinal property, no one really seems to know for sure. I certainly cannot remember, having caught thousands of tench over the years, catching one with wounds which have not healed over.

In a particular, very shallow estate lake that I fish in north Norfolk for instance, where the owner's son regularly water skis thoughout the summer, it is nothing out of the ordinary to catch tench with horrendous wounds across their bodies. Some of these may well be the

With their incredibly thick coating of body mucus, which homogenizes broken tissue quickly, tench are able to survive horrendous injuries, whether caused by a pike attack, or, as in this case, the propellor of an outboard motor.

results of attack by large pike, which the lake is known to contain, but a percentage I am sure are propeller wounds from a powerful outboard engine. Yet in all cases these lacerations are perfectly healed and homogenized in that thick layer of body mucus for which the tench is renowned. Species such as roach or bream have scales that are dislodged easily through bad handling or from predator attack, with the possibility of secondary infection setting in and maybe even premature death. The tench, however, has the tiniest of flat scales, deeply embedded in a tough skin and coated in protective slime of the most tenacious rubberized texture.

Everything about the tench suggests strength and durability – its thick-set, oval body shape, incredibly large, rounded fins and particularly thick tail root. Small wonder they fight so doggedly. The males appear noticeably chunky and shorter than the females, and are easily distinguishable by their 'crinkly' spoon-shaped pelvic fins, the second ray of which is enlarged, and by the lumpy muscles or 'gonads' just above the pelvic fin. When gently compressed against the body the pelvics completely hide the male's vent, whereas the neater, almost pointed pelvic fins of the female do not. The mouth, which if anything is upward pointing (one reason why tench must stand on

It is easier to distinguish between the sexes with tench than any other species. Look at the crinkly pelvic fins that cover the vent and almost touch the anal fin in the male on the left, with lumpy protruding muscles or gonads immediately above. Then compare with the smooth, classic lines of the female on the right.

their heads when feeding from the bottom – see 'Feeding') with thick-rimmed rubber lips, has a tiny barbel at each corner and is semi-protrusible.

Situated in the back of its throat are the powerful pharyngeal teeth used for mincing larger food items into pulp for swallowing. Maggots, for instance, which reappear as mere skins have obviously been crushed by the pharyngeal teeth, the soft insides sucked out and the unwanted parts (including your hook) spat out, even though the bite was not identified at the time. Because these teeth are never seen (unless you cut them from a decaying fish) most anglers would perhaps not realize tench are so equipped. But like all cyprinids (even gudgeon and dace have them), tench could not masticate their food without these flatish plates of bone, which are not dissimilar to those of the crucian carp.

Tench are a decidedly lethargic, ponderous fish. They

thrive best in stillwaters, slow-moving stretches of
lowland rivers, canals, drains and so on, especially where
vegetation is dense, because from soft weeds it obtains
much of its natural diet – insect larvae, snails, shrimps,
anellus, water boatmen, and so on. It also gorges on free-
roaming zooplanktons such as daphnia, the largest of the
water fleas, and is well equipped to siphon through the
detritus, that first few inches of decaying bottom vegetation, in search of annelid worms and midge larvae (see
'Feeding'). It never seems to be bothered by the lack of
oxygen down amongst the silt, and is probably more
tolerant of low levels of dissolved oxygen than any other
freshwater species.

A curiosity regarding the tench, and a question I am
often asked, is how long do they live. Similar to other
cyprinids, such as carp and bream, tench are known to
grow (in length that is) for anything up to 12–15 years.
Once they have stopped growing, and a length of 25–26 in
seems to be around the optimum length for the species
(although most average between 18–22 in), there is nothing
to say that like carp tench do not carry on living for a
further 15–20 years, maybe even longer. So a realistic life
span of 25–30 years should therefore not be discounted.

I am of the opinion that many of the tench inhabiting
certain broads and shallow estate lakes that I have fished
regularly throughout the last 20 years are the very same
tench I encountered when I first fished there. Their average
size of between 4 lb and 6 lb fluctuates a little each year due
to the availability of natural food at the time, and of course
if they spawn particularly late the females weigh considerably more than they did the previous year at around the
same time. And these seasonal weight fluctuations are
probably the reason why we tend not to consider that they
are indeed the same lovely old tench being caught year
after year, just as we have learnt to recognize carp as
individuals. They even look old, some are decidedly
battle-scarred, with marks and nodules on their lips from
being repeatedly caught over the years and healed lacerations from past encounters with herons and pike.

Whilst talking about tench being taken by pike, I have
over the years experienced numerous attacks even when
playing large fish. I remember one particular occasion in
the early 1970s when tench fishing Beeston Lake near

Wroxham (which at one time held the British bream record for a monster of 13 lb 9 oz caught by Mike Davison) when right out of the blue a huge pike grabbed the tench I was playing and it was no small one at that – it looked to be all of 6 lb plus (at that time it would probably have been the largest I had ever caught from Beeston). As it swirled on the surface in 3 ft of water just beyond the rod tip, almost ready for netting, from the corner of one eye I suddenly noticed a huge furrow appear in the weedy margins to my right. The furrow headed straight for the tench, there was an almighty boil on the surface whereupon the line suddenly went limp and then all went calm. I stood there absolutely dumb-founded, and I am sure several seconds elapsed before my brain registered the obvious. I just couldn't believe that such a large specimen as a 6 lb plus tench could be grabbed by a pike, but it had been and I was furious.

There is, however, a happy ending to the story. I was so incensed at the pike that I caught some small rudd to wobble as deadbaits and tried to catch it, actually landing three double-figure pike within as many minutes. Each was particularly thin, almost on the starvation line and weighed a good third less than they should have. Two weighed around 12 lb a piece and the biggest a shade under 19 lb. At 44 in long I should perhaps have been looking at a near 30-pounder, for its head was simply enormous. Obviously the big tench had managed (as most do) to slip away from its grip, unless I caught the wrong pike, which is doubtful because I took a few more emaciated fish and moved the whole lot to nearby Barton Broad where they would be most appreciated and hopefully regain their weight loss. And the 44 in-long tench-grabber was by far the largest.

As a point of interest, the reason that the entire pike stock decided to diet simultaneously was one of simple lack of food. The club who controlled the fishing at Beeston, which the previous year was so full of roach and rudd up to the pound, found that their members were not getting their baits through to the tench, and decided to even the odds by having some of the shoal fish removed. The trouble was that being a small, shallow lake it was easy to net and unbeknown to the club the netman must have removed 99 per cent of the fodder fish, resulting a

The capture of massive tench of 7 and even 8 lb is now considered an everyday event from certain southern reservoirs and gravel pits. However, catches like this quintet of lift-caught beauties weighing between 3½ and 5½ lb are what tench fishing is all about.

few months later in the starving pike attacking anything which moved.

Another curiosity that has occurred only during the last decade or so is the fact that in a fair proportion of fisheries tench are now attaining very much larger weights than ever before – the current British record being a monster of 14 lb 3 oz caught by Phil Gooriah from Wrasbury pits in 1987. For instance, for over 30 years up until 1963 the tench record had slowly increased from 7 lb to just over 9 lb. Yet as I write this, tench of 7 lb and 8 lb are everyday catches in certain southern fisheries, particularly the rich gravel pits in Kent, Hertfordshire and Oxfordshire.

For a high-value specimen these days enthusiasts in the know are looking towards tench of 9 lb plus, a fish which, as I have said, 30 years ago would have broken the record.

Lots of theories have been put forward as to why this is happening, of course. The favourite is that the huge quantities of high-nutritional-value paste and boiled baits that have been introduced (initially to attract carp), and which the tench have subsequently learnt to accept as natural food, has resulted in their growing very much larger. Certainly, the number of tench taken nowadays

over 9 lb and 10 lb is completely mind-boggling; it is rather strange to anglers who have been around long enough to monitor the scene for the last 30 or 40 years, because it has all happened so comparatively recently and with only tench, no other species.

However, is it really all down to the high-nutritional-value (HNV) baits? I have my doubts about this. Certainly the fluctuating seasons and weather patterns we are now

Females that are still carrying spawn during the early season should be handled with extreme care. They could possibly weigh as much as 2–3 lb more than their natural body weight.

With distinct black eyes and irregular black flecks over a bright yellow body, the rare golden tench is nicknamed 'banana fish'. Strangely, it does not appear to hybridize with the common green tench, and exists in only a handful of fisheries within the British Isles.

experiencing on a global scale surely have some bearing on the matter, although it's difficult to isolate a direct link other than because the summers on average start later, more tench are caught at the beginning of the season so grossly over-full with spawn they weigh considerably heavier than their natural weight, probably by 2–3 lb.

To counter-balance this view, completely spawned-out tench of 8 lb and 9 lb are regularly taken every year nowadays from some of the Kent gravel pits. So where are we? What is even more interesting and in complete contrast to gravel pit fisheries, where the tench may well have reached far greater weight partly through feeding regularly on HNV baits, is the fact that reservoirs like the Tring group in Hertfordshire, which are rich only in zoo planktons and other completely natural foods, are now producing more tench in excess of that magical 10 lb barrier than any other fisheries. And these are waters which have *not* been mass baited over a period of years with HNV carp baits. So exactly why tench are now averaging much larger weights in a selection of fisheries spread over southern England I shall leave you to puzzle out. At least the phenomenon pinpoints waters where these jumbo fish are to be found. Not that any of this makes the slightest bit of real difference to the enjoyment of catching tench as a species, because even 2- and 3-pounders will, on the right tackle, put up an exciting fight. Fish of between 4 and 5 lb are the backbone of quality tench fishing and should always be regarded as such. And personally I still rate tench of 5 lb plus as the realistic goal to aim for. Remember we are talking here in terms of general tench fishing.

GOLDEN TENCH

This beautiful, quite breathtaking creature is more an aquariast's fish than an angler's quarry, though it does exist in a handful of fisheries around the country, particularly those without large predators like pike, which is not difficult to understand. To a predator the golden tench right from the fry stage must stand out like the proverbial sore thumb, just like albino fish, so their survival rate with

every creature trying to get in on the act, including the
ever-watchful heron, must be miniscule.

Often nicknamed 'banana fish', the golden tench is
indeed the colour of a ripe banana even down to the black
spots irregularly flecked over its body, though I have seen
a fair number of golden tench completely free of any dark
markings. It also sports a black eye, pink, translucent,
rather petite fins, and overall a much slimmer profile than
the common green tench. It is thus by comparison a poor
fighter, nowhere near so powerful, though dogged nonetheless. Optimum size rarely exceeds 3 lb and this is large
for the golden tench.

As with green tench the males are distinguishable from
the females by their spoon-shaped pelvic fins and the
lumpy muscles or gonads immediately above them.

Strangely the two types, green and golden, to the best of
my knowledge do not inter-breed or throw up mutants.
Occasionally one catches a green tench etched with purple
markings or blotches all over its head and body. But these I
have always taken to be colour disorders in the pigmenta-
tion rather like purplish birth marks. Such markings have
nothing to do with inter-breeding between golden and
green tench.

CHAPTER TWO

ABOUT TENCH

FEEDING

Compared to carp for example, especially when living alongside and therefore in direct competition with them, tench come a poor second in making full use of the natural food at their disposal. They are by nature nowhere near so aggressive, and in reality are probably the most deliberate feeders of all freshwater fish. For tench to grow large they require an exceptionally rich environment, and only in such circumstances are both tench and carp able to attain huge proportions living together. Even then tench still need to outnumber the carp. Switched the other way around, carp will eat them out of house and home.

On really heavily stocked carp fisheries with next to no weed from which the tench can eek a living, and where the water is kept in a continual state of turbidity from the sheer number of carp feeding from the bottom at various times of the day, tench may not even be able to exist beyond a weight of 1 lb or so. Miniature tench of a few ounces seem able to grow amongst densely stocked carp because their infant food requirements are different. But once they require larger food particles higher up the chain, carp rule the roost and the tench can never reach anywhere near their full growth potential. Even adult tench of fully 2 to 3 lb purchased from fish farmers by clubs and lake-owners for stocking into densely populated carp fisheries can never compete. Inevitably they become thinner and thinner, barely scratching a living and merely surviving at half their normal body weight (and it is surprising just how thin tench can become) before being reduced to starvation by the carp. Obviously, these are uncommon circumstances but events I have witnessed on a handful of club waters where the members have thought a second species was needed without realizing the consequences.

As tench kindly pin-point their position when feeding heavily at dawn by sending up patches of tiny bubbles, the best way of locating them is to scan the surface with binoculars.

Having located tench bubbling close into the marginal weeds of this large gravel pit, wheelchair angler Robbie Robertson finds the successful method is to pole-fish a single caster just above the bottom weed beneath a waggler.

In the two small carp lakes that I control, for instance, both densely populated with carp and catfish up to 20 lb, the tench grow thick and chunky-looking up to about 12 oz and are perfectly healthy, but never get any bigger. I suppose the tench is just too slow and ponderous for its own good.

The nice thing about tench when they are feeding in earnest is that they often (though not always) send bubbles up to the surface to tell you where they are. If you watch the surface very carefully (never forget the binoculars – even for close-range observation they are indispensible) the route of each individual fish can usually be followed simply by relating to the groups of bubbles as they appear. In heavily pre-baited swims full of numbers of fish all moving agitatedly about, when the surface looks to all intents and purposes like a witches' cauldron, this just isn't possible. But in swims occupied by just a handful of tench, following the bubbles of individuals can prove almost as fascinating as hooking into one of them. Wherever strong-limbed trees overhang the swim, endeavour to reach a position overhead where you can look directly into the area (providing the water is clear) and observe the stream of bubbles rising from the tench. It teaches you so much about the fish's behaviour. There are in fact various kinds of bubbles attributed to tench which rise to the surface and you must learn to identify them. The tiny 'needle' bubbles made by the tench itself, which escape through its gill filaments as a result of it masticating its food, are perhaps the easiest to identify. Large patches of frothy bubbles, on the other hand, gases released from rotten vegetation in silty waters by the tench in their search for blood-worms, (midge larvae) their favourite natural food, just might be the work of carp or eels. So beware, even experienced anglers come to grief with these gas bubbles on occasion, and view anything 'frothy' with an open mind.

Tench also send up small groups of bubbles in clusters of just two or three, five or six at a time when they are feeding over hard gravel. These are noticeably smaller than those produced by carp, and so there should be little confusion. They are made when the tench stands on its head to suck up baits one at a time and rights itself to chew them, thus emitting only a limited amount. It then moves on a foot or so to the next food item (a grain of corn, piece of flake, etc) and another small group of bubbles rise upwards.

The interpretation and identification of bubbles, and matching them to particular fish, is almost a separate hobby. So try whenever you are given the opportunity to observe tench feeding in crystal-clear water. As an experiment, take a landing-net pole or a bank stick and watch what happens on the surface when you rupture the detritus, that decaying top layer of bottom silt, just as a tench might do when it characteristically stands on its head and with a thrust of its tail runs its nose along the bottom to dislodge and throw up particles of natural food. This of course is why raking or dragging a silty swim proves so effective (pp. 81–84) the tench has its work done for it.

Tench are unquestionably at their most difficult to tempt when they are preoccupied on microscopic food items, in particular zooplankton such as daphnia. There is no mistaking this transparent water flea whose body is tinged a red-brown colour. When it is blown into the margins by wind drift or a strong underwater tow, the concentrations are so thick it's impossible to see the bottom even through gin-clear water. It appears to all intents and purposes as though the water is littered with brick dust. And during the warmer months when daphnia multiplies rapidly, it is to tench what krill is to whales.

I have witnessed numbers of tench lying idly on the bottom of warm, clear, shallow water along margins that are stacked with huge daphnia concentrations, simply gorging themselves completely oblivious to any other food item. I have, believe it or not, lowered a single maggot on an 18 hook tied direct to 2 lb line on to their noses and watched in sheer amazement as it tumbled over the lips and down to the bottom, cast after cast, without the slightest interest being shown. It was as if the maggot did not exist. A bunch of brandlings was given similar treatment, although eventually I did on one occasion 'tweak' at what must have been the right moment, for the tench promptly sucked them in.

Then again, as they were lying there drinking in a gullet-full of daphnia with every breath, perhaps the worms simply went in with the fleas. The area was shared with several large eels also gorging on daphnia, and each similarly positioned, tails stabilized in the silt and their

bodies held in suspension off the bottom like serpents. I would never have believed that eels could by nature refuse a bunch of fresh worms, but these did. As with the tench, even when the worms were lowered on to the eels' gaping mouths, it was as though they were invisible. Such was the draw of and preoccupation with daphnia.

So frustrated was I by this chain of events that on the following morning I went armed with a small mesh aquarium net, a packet of aspic and a flask of hot water. A netful of solid daphnia was soon gathered and put into the bottom of a 2-pt bait tin together with the powdered aspic and water from the flask. After 20 minutes the mixture was well set. I cut my block of daphnia jelly into ¾ in cubes and slipped one gently on to a size 8 hook. I would love to report that at this point Wilson went on to bag up with 'plump' impossible tench on these daphnia cubes, but I am afraid this is not the case. The wind changed overnight and took with it both tench and daphnia to a distant spot; they were too far away for the cubes to be lowered in, and the super-soft cubes cannot stand up to casting. I had this wonderful idea that all I had to do was lower the cube, which looked exactly what it was, a clear concentration of daphnia, on to the nose of a gorging tench and in it would go. Ah well. It seemed a good idea at the time; and if a similar situation ever arose again, I would go through the same rigmarole.

Opposite: *The tench of large clear-water pits and lakes gather wherever the wind and sub-surface tow drifts massive concentrations of daphnia. When gorging themselves close into the margins on these nutritious water fleas, the tench are not distracted even by the continuous passing of water-skiers.*

REPRODUCTION

It is the customary close season worry of coarse fishermen throughout England and Wales (no close seasons in Ireland and Scotland, remember) every year as each new season approaches – will the tench have spawned by 16th June or not?

And of course in the vast majority of waters, even shallow lakes and ponds which warm up quickly, they rarely have. In over 30 years of tench fishing I cannot ever remember starting a new season on 16 June at any fishery where the whole tench population had completed its reproduction cycle. There have been isolated years when, due to an incredibly warm spring and more importantly a period of warm nights during late May and early June, which raises water temperatures sufficiently to stimulate spawning, a large percentage of a particular fishery's tench population has indeed shed most of their eggs and milt by mid-June. However, I can only relate to the lake I was concentrating my efforts upon at that time.

Perhaps mother nature has intended that tench should take a long time about reproduction and stagger egg-laying over a period of several weeks regardless of water temperature, to allow for an early lack of soft weed growth, a proponderance of small predators (such as perch), and inclement June weather when sudden over-night frosts dampen everyone's enthusiasm, not just for spawning tench. Besides, the tench species is so incredibly strong (fortunately) that as long as the pot-bellied females are handled carefully, no harm will come to them or their eggs. Nonetheless, I do think that whoever suggested 16 June as an opportune date to end the close season was rather ill advised because in deep, cold gravel pits the tench may not be stimulated into spawning until as late as the end of July. Or were the seasons so very different, say, a hundred years ago? We shall never really know, because most gravel-pit tench fisheries were dug after World War II.

Courtship begins with groups of males, from two up to several at a time, following the females; four or five males all vying for the attentions of a single female is not out of the ordinary. Actual egg-laying sometimes continues throughout the entire day and night, but generally early mornings are chosen. The sudden change in air temper-ature at that time of day is enough to stimulate a response from the female. She spreads the sticky carpet of eggs through the weeds while the males disperse their milky white milt to fertilize them. As their quiet nature suggests, tench are nowhere near so noisy as carp when propagating their species. They prefer to lay their eggs (unlike carp) in the thickest clumps of soft weeds they can find, and even in the carpets of crunchy, bright green surface algae which dog the surface during summer when water levels are low and there are long periods of bright sunshine.

I remember during the heatwave of 1976, when my brother, David, and I were tench fishing in a large, beautiful, shallow estate lake in North Norfolk, finding by accident thousands upon thousands of 1 to 2 in long tench fry blown to the dam end of the lake amongst the remains of a huge carpet of algae. Unfortunately, the heavy rain which fell continuously throughout that August Bank Holiday weekend had reduced the floating algae almost to nothing. Strangely, the lake contained next to no soft weed beds that year, and the tench had only the algae to use as a spawning cover. What had drawn my attention to the dam end initially was the sight of a large eel gorging itself on surface fry in the shallows by the outlet, which I could see through binoculars from our swim some 100 yd away. When I went to see what was happening I observed more young tench than I have ever seen, either before or since. I rather think most of them fell prey to the eels, perch, and inevitably gulls and herons.

Each female carries an enormous amount of eggs – up to, and even over, one quarter of its body weight – which is why a 9½ lb female can easily tip the scales at over 12 lb when full of spawn. Once the tiny translucent eggs hatch, after 6–10 days, the alevins are initially reliant on yolk from the egg. They then feed on microscopic planktons amongst the weed in which they hide. Anglers may not come into contact with the small tench for at least several years. In most fisheries the young stay in the weed, feeding on minute aquatic life, and rarely come into contact with an angler's bait. From about 1 lb upwards, the tench seems willing to leave the sanctity of weed for long periods and join its larger brethren in small groups, by which time it is liable to suck in food containing a hook.

DISTRIBUTION

Within the British Isles the tench is even more widely spread than carp. While they are not exactly common in Scotland, tench are distributed throughout England and Wales with tremendous concentrations all over Ireland. They have a natural preference for ponds, pits, lakes, meres, broads and reservoirs, but there are few rivers which do not harbour at least a few tench. They are so prolific in the slow-moving Lincolnshire drains and throughout the Great Ouse system, for instance, that a

Comfortably and strategically placed to cover tench as they move through a narrow deep channel connecting one pit to another, this angler offers sweetcorn on the lift rig.

Tench waters come in all shapes and sizes from massive, wind-swept gravel pits where long-range ledgering is often the order of the day, to diminutive, over-grown, secluded lakes where float-fishing beneath the rod tip amongst the lilies offers the best prospects.

good bag of river tench is very likely from any number of locations. Even well-known fast rivers like the Hampshire Avon contain tench, and periodically tench even choose to occupy fast-running areas. Weir pools in particular hold a special attraction during the summer months and whenever the river is in flood. The tench has also been stocked into North American waters and those of Australasia.

CHAPTER THREE

LOCATING TENCH

I HAVE already described how tench give away their position by sending tiny feeding bubbles up to the surface, and a more exact, instant method of locating them does not exist. It is also true to say, however, that even with a fair-sized group of tench packed tightly into a relatively small area, they do not always bubble. It is imperative, therefore, that you know the type of habitats they prefer in various kinds of waters if you wish to catch tench with consistency. Make no mistake: there really is no substitute for learning the craft of observation at the waterside. There is invariably a visual pointer when tench are present, no matter what the conditions, although a situation such as continual really heavy rain can make it difficult to identify. Even on decidedly 'off days', however, when there is little feeling of activity and a complete lack of surface bubbles, there will be a sign or two of tench activity somewhere: reed stalks 'knocking', a sudden but distinctive calm patch amid a rippled surface, the rounded head and shoulders of a tench silently porpoising, patches of discoloured water, rocking lily pads, and so on.

These are just a few of your pointers, so don't forget the binoculars. You will be able to observe things with them that it is not possible to see with the naked eye. Heavy, extremely powerful binoculars are more of a hindrance than a help, because after a while their weight around the neck becomes unbearable, and they spend the rest of the day back in their case. Ideally, you want a lightweight pair with a magnification of 8 × 30 or 10 × 40, which can be hung around the neck all day if required without discomfort. There they are to hand at a moment's notice so that you can observe sudden surface disturbances in soft weed-beds or among lilies, locate sudden eruptions of bubbles beyond the swim being fished, and keep track of tench should they move on. Binoculars are very much a working tool and should be used as such. No one should set off fishing for species like carp, bream and tench, which portray their presence by surface activity, without them.

It goes without saying that a pair of polaroid glasses are another indispensable part of the tench fisherman's armoury. Those with 'yellow' lenses are good because they polarize and cut out reflective glare from the surface, and brighten the existing light by a couple of stops. For dull days, or during periods of low light such as dawn and dusk, yellow polaroids really are a terrific aid.

STILLWATER HABITATS

Many facets of watercraft are directly linked to location, and one of the most interesting (for some almost a hobby in itself) is the study of water plants. As tench are never far from vegetation when given the choice, locate their favourite habitats and you have located tench. It's as simple as that. As small waters such as ponds and pits are a microcosm of much larger sheets of water, because each will in fact contain similar features, similar plants, and be overhung by similar trees, an understanding of the natural history of ponds and gravel pits will stand you in good stead for locating tench wherever you fish. For example, knowledge of the kind of bottom strata preferred by a particular plant will tell you the nature of the bottom in that area of water, be it soft or hard.

Reeds

Tall species of grass such as the common reed (often referred to as the Norfolk reed because it is commonly used for thatching in that county), which attracts tench like flies to a honey pot, cannot grow in really soft silt, or it would soon be uprooted in strong winds. So reeds grow thickest where the bottom is generally of a firm structure, such as in gravel, marl or clay.

During the early season the reeds with green, round stems, which may each grow to 10 ft high, can often be

Find thick beds of the tall common reed lining the margins of a lake, mere, pond or pit and you will have found tench. They can readily be caught on float tackle with the bait presented on the bottom close alongside or actually between small gaps in the reeds.

seen 'twitching', 'clanging' or 'swaying' when there is no wind, as tench either brush the stems as they move between them, or remove crustaceans and aquatic insect larvae such as the caddis grub.

One of my favourite tench waters, Alderfen Broad near Wroxham, has an irregular line of tall reeds along one entire shoreline, and invariably as dawn breaks odd clusters of bubbles can be seen alongside them. To cast a bait between the reeds into bays and narrow channels that reach no further than a couple of feet into the reeds often brings an instant, dramatic response. There is certainly never any dallying. The tench takes the bait with all the confidence in the world and so it should, amongst the reeds it is feeding at home.

Reed mace

Another reed with a liking for a firmish bottom in which to anchor its thick, fibrous roots is the greater reed mace, best known for its large, brown, cigar-like seed heads.

Often called the bullrush (wrongly), the reed mace and the lesser reed mace (a slimmer plant) both attract tench in numbers, particularly during the early season when water temperatures are high. The fibrous-matting type roots at the base are much favoured by spawning tench, which regularly return throughout the following days to mop up their own and the spawn of others.

This angler uses the cover of marginal grasses to present float-fished brandlings alongside the dark, onion-stemmed bull-rushes where tench are working.

Beds of reed mace which make the best tench hot spots are those with their roots in marginal depths of between 2 and 3 ft. Because the stems do not grow so close together as those of the common reed, even large tench may just pass between without so much as a shudder on the brown seed heads. So keep a sharp lookout for tail patterns, or bubbles on the surface amongst the stems.

Bullrush

The true bullrush with its dark green, distinctly onion-like stems, tapering gradually to a fine tip is more commonly found in flowing water. However, it does grow happily in

fertile, clear-watered ponds, lakes and pits, where the
bottom is guaranteed to attract a prolific colony of
freshwater shrimps – and thus tench.

Sweet reed grass

This tall, rush-like marginal prefers a soft bottom where its
creeping rootstock form such a dense mass you might be
led into thinking you are treading on dry ground, until
your boot suddenly fills up. It hangs out over the margins
with as much as 3 to 4 ft of water beneath the dark floating
canopy, and is much loved by tench. They can be caught
directly under the rod tip when patrolling amongst the
extensive sub-surface rootstock, which harbours delicacies
such as midge larvae, leeches, snails, beetles, caddis and the
like.

So much for the more popular 'tench attracting' marginal
plants – now let us consider soft weeds and then floating
plants.

Soft weeds

These, the submerged oxygenating plants like Canadian
pond weed, hornwort, mill foil, can pose enormous
problems in clear water where, due to the maximum
penetration of sunlight, they grow rampant. And generally
speaking the smaller the pond or pit, the more rampant
and the more problematic they become. It's often possible
to observe bubbles from tench (feeding down on the
bottom, beneath the weed) rise to cluster tantalizingly on
the surface without there being a way of getting the bait
down to them.

Tench are naturally attracted by the overhead protection
and diffused light that these soft weeds provide, and of
course to the larder of aquatic insect larvae attached to their
stems.

To present the bait to tench close into the margins, clear
channels or holes need first to be dragged (pp. 81–84), so
do not be deterred even about areas that are completely
choked and seemingly unfishable. Such swims will (after
clearing) allow presentation of the bait on light float tackle,
the nicest way of all to catch tench.

Surface plants

Tench love to occupy areas beneath lilies. As for many
species, the attraction is a roof over their heads, diffusing
the light and obscuring enemies. In such places tench
always feel comfortable to browse and feed in their
characteristically ponderous, lazy way, even through the
heat and brightness of a summer day, when they abandon
more open swims as the sun starts to rise high in the sky.

There really is no better day-time retreat in which to
locate tench than beneath surface plants. The first 4 lb
tench I ever caught came on a bamboo roach pole from
beneath surface cover, although the cover was not what
you might expect. It did not consist of lilies but an old
wooden door (the pit was being back-filled with builders
rubble and the like), and from beneath one side of the
floating door I could clearly see through polaroid glasses
the protruding tails of several large fish. The tails looked in
fact to belong to chub, but when I lowered a large lump of
flake down beside the edge of the door on a small
weightless waggler rig, it suddenly disappeared and I was
playing a 4 lb tench which led me a fine song and dance for
several minutes on just 3 lb test line. Strangely enough I
went on to take a further two tench, both smaller than the
first, plus a nice roach from beneath that door, all in an
hour's fishing. This illustrates perfectly the value of
floating cover, even if the roach pole and fixed line was a
trifle cavalierish.

To tackle thick lily beds with inadequate tackle or even
the wrong type of outfit (such as a fast-taper rod instead of
one with a forgiving, cushioning action) could be asking
for trouble. What proves invaluable, however, is an
understanding of the structure of stems and roots beneath a
mass of floating pads and flowers.

Whilst there are numerous cultivated varieties of coloured
lilies available only a handful of clubs or owners plant their
fisheries with them. This is a pity because it's impossible to
make a stillwater fishery look too beautiful, and to sit
catching tench with pink or dark red lilies dotted amongst
a carpet of velvet-green pads is a delightful experience.

There are no less than five commonly found 'natural' lily
type plants which attract tench: the common yellow

All tench fishermen share a love/hate relationship with soft weeds like the Canadian pond weed. It provides shade above the tench's heads in addition to a larder of aquatic insects, and so encourages clear-water tench to work close into the margins. But in thick beds it creates snags from which it is impossible to extract a hooked tench. There is then only one answer: dragging.

water-lily, sometimes referred to as brandy bottle due to the distinctive shape of the seed head, which forms once the petals have shed; the common white water-lily (the white alba lily); the dwarf pond lily: broad-leaved pond weed; and amphibious bistort.

Tench adore the *common yellow lily* because of its soft, cabbage-like, sub-surface leaves, amongst which they love to browse. Most anglers often refer to this plant simply as 'cabbages', especially in certain river systems where the pads and flowers rarely reach the surface. Boating activity can be responsible for this, as can, to some degree, excessive depth. It is one and the same lily, nonetheless.

The root structure of the common yellow water-lily, with its accompanying sub-surface, lettuce-type leaves, is so enormous and fast-spreading that clubs organize working parties to thin the beds out. Below the mass of surface pads and flowers is a quiet area of diffused light where tench feel at home.

In shallow lakes, however, particularly those with a bottom layer rich in nutrients, the sheer growth of both sub-surface cabbage and floating pads can present a daunting prospect when you are thinking of extracting tench. Nevertheless, present a bait close to or actually amongst the soft leaves, and tench will not be far away.

Second in both size and root structure density to the common yellow lily comes the *white alba lily* and the cultivated hybrids. Due to their very much smaller rhizomes, thinner stalks and complete absence of sub-surface greenery, there is naturally more room beneath the pads and beautiful flowers for tench to both hide and move about, although viewed from the surface the growth looks impenetrable.

The *dwarf pond lily* is not really a true lily, although its small, round green pads and buttercup-yellow flowers would fool most fishermen. The main difference between it and the true lilies (a most useful fact to the tench angler) is that it multiplies rapidly, not by sending up extra stalks and pads from the bottom roots, but by growing outwards

Thick beds of dwarf pond lily help to shade the surface in clear-watered gravel pits, encouraging tench to feed confidently close in along the marginal shelf. This permits simple float-fishing techniques, such as the lift, to be used.

in short bursts across the surface. It creates mini plants each with its own rootstock and flowerhead, every 6–10 in. At the end of the summer these little plants rot off and separate from the old main stem; they drift into the margins where a percentage take hold. And in the following spring, it all sprouts up again. This lily also spreads from the seed head once the yellow flowers die off.

It is by far the fastest-spreading surface plant after duck weed, and it attracts tench in numbers. One advantage of this plant, when you are trying to extract fish from a seemingly impossible surface covering, (see 'Raking') is that while the long stems and pads are tough and thick on the surface, there is little beneath the surface for tackle to catch on. A couple of square yards of floating jungle may be supported underneath by only half a dozen thin stalks.

Broad-leaved pond weed is also regularly frequented by tench. In some locations, especially shallow marl, clay and gravel pits, the oval-shaped green leaves (often noticeably crinkly along the edges) can clog the surface almost from bank to bank. It is easily recognizable by the erect, tight, pink seed heads. Also, from the hard bottom in which it prefers to root, the main stem can sub-divide two or three times before each individual plant reaches the surface. For this reason the density of foliage causes a problem only from mid-water upwards. Like most surface plants, broad-leaved pond weed flourishes best in depths of between 2 ft and 6 ft. This is useful to know when you are reconnoitring new waters, because a reasonably accurate assessment of depths can be made wherever this plant covers the surface.

This applies also to *amphibious bistort* which is really a terrestrial plant that loves to have its roots in water, thus providing a floating canopy for tench in depths up to around 3 ft. It, too, sports an erect, knotty, pink seed head, but the leaves are pointed and dark green. It will occasionally grow as a thick covering well out from the bank over gravel bars, but it is more often seen growing in thick clumps along the margins, sprouting on dry land and reaching out across the surface, exactly where you would expect to find tench browsing.

During the heat of a summer's day, especially when tench feel vulnerable in clear water and are loathe to be seen out in the open, the best place to search is around surface-covering plants.

Hidden sub-surface features

So much for locating tench by visually identifying those plants they most like to frequent, and in part treat as home. But what about lakes, ponds or pits which, for one reason or another, remain weedless for much, perhaps all of the summer – waters without obvious features where the tench might be anywhere. Gravel pits are renowned for their uneven sub-surface contours, created when the sand and gravel deposits were originally laid down following the last Ice Age. To harvest the maximum potential in minerals, aggregate companies dig deeper into the richest seams, thus creating gullies or holes once the pit has been allowed to fill from the water table (fig. 1).

It is along these deeper gullies, or in the holes and drop-offs that tench love to patrol. The bottom lay-out is to them as avenues, cul-de-sacs and road systems appear to us. Obviously, time spent carefully plummetting un-known waters to gain a mental picture of the bottom contours will prevent you wasting time when you are fishing. Make a sketch of each fishery you visit, and draw in the deeper areas so that you have a record for next time.

After spending numerous sessions at a particular pit, it will become obvious that tench frequent certain areas only at certain times of the day. In clear-watered pits, for instance, it usually follows that marginal ledges and gullies are favoured during low light levels such as dusk and dawn, when tench are feeding in earnest on natural food. As the light increases, they evacuate the margins in preference for distant deeps, where they may very well spend all the midday hours. Now this is not a rule of thumb, because tench in each water react differently, but wherever there is a complete lack of marginal cover or surface habitats, such as partly submerged overhanging trees or lily-type plants, it is a good yardstick.

Featureless waters

In featureless waters which appear not to contain definite feeding areas or routes, location is purely one of attraction, as is the case with similar species such as bream. In other

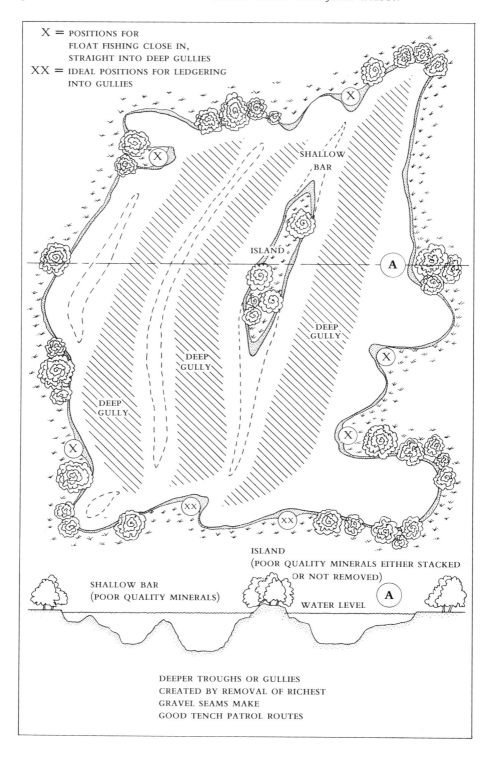

X = POSITIONS FOR
FLOAT FISHING CLOSE IN,
STRAIGHT INTO DEEP GULLIES

XX = IDEAL POSITIONS FOR LEDGERING
INTO GULLIES

SHALLOW
BAR

ISLAND

DEEP
GULLY

DEEP
GULLY

DEEP
GULLY

A

ISLAND
(POOR QUALITY MINERALS EITHER STACKED
OR NOT REMOVED)

SHALLOW BAR
(POOR QUALITY MINERALS)

WATER LEVEL

A

DEEPER TROUGHS OR GULLIES
CREATED BY REMOVAL OF RICHEST
GRAVEL SEAMS MAKE
GOOD TENCH PATROL ROUTES

words, tench are best found by attracting them to an area of your choice by regular pre-baiting (pp. 81–84). Carp anglers know only too well how tench respond to regular helpings of free nosh. In waters with low densities of carp, during the early season especially, tench can actually become a nuisance, pinching the loose feed long before the carp ever find it.

RIVER TENCH

Though comparatively few anglers bother specifically with them, tench in slow, deepish lowland rivers offer an interesting and challenging proposition when they are most active throughout the summer months. The odd fish might even turn up in the winter, especially during and immediately after heavy flooding which has the tendency to wake them up. They are, however, considerably more active in moving water during the warmer months. Years ago my favourite early season tipple was following the bream shoals of the Upper Waveney. This necessitated

A new gravel-pit fishery – perhaps a tench water in the making. The drag-line digs deeper when removing the richest mineral seams, leaving long troughs or gullies. Location of these by careful plummeting of the bottom provides the most likely guide to tench feeding areas and patrol routes.

FIGURE 1 (Opposite) A mature gravel pit seen from surface level and (bottom) a cross section of the same gravel pit showing how gullies and deep holes – the tench patrol routes – are formed

pre-baiting a couple of likely-looking deep holes on the bends between the cabbage patches with mashed bread and bran (half a bucketful) on the night before, in readiness for a dawn start. And nearly always, a couple of tench would come to the net first during half light.

If the bream failed completely to show, then up to half a dozen river tench were on the cards. Those tench would consume most of the free nosh during the hours of darkness in the company of quality roach (a big one happened along occasionally), but unlike the bream would hang around for quite some time afterwards as though they were waiting for more. Thus they were always obliging customers with the dawn chorus.

Had I the presence of mind at that time (I was far more intent on catching bream) to pre-bait several swims with mashed bread, each might have attracted a group of tench by dawn. And by leap-frogging from swim to swim in true roving fashion, giving each about half an hour, a bag of river tench would not have been out of the question.

Numerous opportune tench have come my way over the years from wandering weedy rivers like the Waveney, especially while chub fishing, using polaroid glasses to search among the runs. Once the sun becomes too high for easy, instant chubbing, and eyes can easily pierce the clear water down to the bottom, the dark, ponderous shape of a tench can easily be seen, often 'hovering' well off bottom. Anglers tend to believe that tench spend much of their time on or very close to the bottom, but this is simply not the case. Observation at close quarters allows you to study their behaviour and see the way in which the tench angles downwards and stands on its head to suck up a bait presented hard on the bottom.

Like their stillwater counterparts, river tench love to browse through the soft, cabbage-like leaves of the common yellow water-lily. They might turn up anywhere, but are more liable to frequent choice habitats like beds of lilies. In addition, search deep and weedy mill pools, overshoot pools, confluences where ditches or sidestreams join the main flow creating a depression, deep holes on acute bends, beneath overhanging willows, and so on. These are the areas to concentrate on.

Curiously, I have also caught tench from the deepest water beneath fast-flowing weir pools; however, it is very much quieter down on the bottom and obviously more to their liking. Built to face a fast flow continuously tench are certainly not; conversely, don't be surprised when large baits like a whole lobworm or lump of bread flake intended for bream or chub produces a tench.

WINTER TENCH

In a typical British winter, with occasional falls of snow and stillwaters frozen over during much of the coldest weather, winter tench are not really a worthwhile proposition. Their metabolic rate seems to slow considerably more than that of carp, although where tench share carp fisheries, and so regularly feed on the boilies introduced to keep the carp interested, they are of course far more commonly caught. And during mild spells brought about by mild south-westerly or westerly winds, the odd tench can be expected at some time during the day.

There is a lovely shallow estate lake at Felbrigg Hall in North Norfolk, where I once used to take large bags of specimen winter rudd. It was particularly productive towards the latter part of the season in early March when temperatures were rising, and whenever the stream which feeds the lake and runs through the middle became flooded, artificially colouring the usually quite clear water. Then and only then could winter tench actually be relied upon to show. My brother, Dave, came up to Norfolk from Hertfordshire one weekend on my so-called guarantee of his getting amongst the big rudd, as at that time during a prolonged mild spell they were really feeding in earnest. But all he caught one after another, on a block-end feeder rig baited with maggots, was no less than 13 tench. Now I use the word 'all' with caution, because a bag of 13 tench is lovely at any time. But they were not what Dave had set his sights upon. Incidentally he never did catch a big rudd from the lake.

I use this occasion to illustrate that in the right weather and water conditions combined, winter tench are certainly on the cards, especially from shallow lakes which warm quickly and get them moving about on the look out for food. Simply scale down a bit on summer strengths of line

and hook sizes, and use smaller baits and far less groundbait or loose feed. And be rather more patient when waiting for bites. Otherwise, the techniques and baits do not really change.

Try swims close to habitats which offer some kind of protection, such as overhanging or partly submerged trees, or amongst the rotting roots where summer lily-beds once graced the surface. Tench will still be around there even in winter.

Deep weir pools hold enormous attraction for tench. This plump 4-pounder accepted John's ledgered bread flake in the middle of a roach and bream haul taken during filming of the TV series, Go Fishing, made on the River Wensum.

River tench turn up at the most unlikely times. This 3-pounder gobbled up a worm intended for chub in a backwater of Hertfordshire's River Lea, and provided a bonus winter catch for John's brother.

CHAPTER FOUR

TACKLE

WHILE it is true that even quality tench are sometimes landed on the finest tackle used by match
fishermen, an unacceptable proportion come off when this
type of set-up is used. Either the tiny hook pulls out, the
tackle snags up in weed-beds resulting in a break-off, or the
power of the fish snaps the fine hook link. Conversely,
tench of all sizes are regularly taken by carp fishermen on
tackle which is vastly overgunned in relation to them.
Nobody, for instance, could possibly enjoy cranking in a
3 lb tench hooked on a heavy-bomb shock rig and 10 lb or
12 lb test line.

The result of both these situations (either too light or too
heavy tackle), which are common everyday occurrences, is
that the tench is rarely enjoyed to the full by a large
proportion of anglers. I know numerous young carp
fishermen who never have a good word to say about tench
simply because they have never geared their tackle to suit
and fished specifically for them. The fight of any fish,
tench included, can only ever be related to the tackle being
used to subdue it. So please consider carefully the
following pages about tackle choice, and the tench without
question will become a firm summer favourite.

RODS

At a pinch almost any general-purpose fibre-glass match or
float rod of between 11 ft and 14 ft long or ledger rod of
9 ft to 11 ft will suffice for catching tench. Many situations
can be happily tackled with these two, although inevitably
they will not cover every situation.

As with many items of tackle which have been designed
for a specific purpose, rods particularly suited to catching
tench are more desirable and more versatile. And there is a
wonderful choice in lightweight but robust carbon models

which will allow you to control even the largest fish, while permitting full enjoyment from the ensuing fight whatever size the tench happens to be. So let us consider some of the options.

Float rods

For fishing out into deep water or over beds of marginal lilies with lines up to 4 lb and 5 lb test, choose a good-quality, three-piece 13 ft carbon match rod (a 14-footer if most of your tench fishing will be in deep water). Do not get one with an ultra-fine, spliced tip designed for fishing the stick float with ultra-light hook lengths, because inevitably the tip will snap off.

A 'waggler'-style rod, crisp in action for hitting tiny dips of the float, yet with a 'cushioning' bend throughout, is perfect for the job. Those strengthened with wraps of 'kevlar' are highly recommended.

As lines of up to 5 lb may be used, ask the tackle-dealer to suggest a rod which is not unduly thin in the wall thickness. It is far better to settle for one which weighs a shade more, than to be worrying about a super-lightweight model snapping off when you bend into a tench bent on wrapping the line around lily roots.

When contemplating extracting tench on the float from extremely snaggy close-in situations like dense lily-beds or beside the woodwork of submerged willow branches, where the possibility exists of hooking into really large fish on a break or bust tussle, a carbon match rod is definitely not the tool for the job. This is where a two-piece, 12 ft carbon fibre, 'Avon'-actioned specialist rod is required – one with a test curve of around 1¼ lb, so that it will handle lines from 5 lb to 7½ lb comfortably. The test curve of any rod is the pull required to bend the tip of the rod into a quarter circle, measured in pounds. You then simply multiply that figure (1¼ lb) by 5 to arrive at the ideal line strength – 6¼ lb. You then multiply by 4 (5 lb) and then by 6 (7½ lb) to give guidelines to the rod's lowest and highest limits. This is not to say that much lower hook lengths, for instance, cannot be used with such a rod, because when distance fishing in snag-free conditions with less torque on the outfit, you will be able to fish quite fine, even down to, say, a 3 lb hook link.

This youngster is enjoying the fight of a tench hooked at close range using the right rod for the job: a two-piece, all-through-action Avon.

Ledger rods

The very same Avon-actioned carbon rod with a 1¼ lb test curve is the perfect all-round tool to catch tench when freelining or ledgering. For close range work an 11-footer is sufficient; whereas for picking up more line on the strike in order to hit tiny bites at range, say distances of 40 to 50 yd plus, the extra length of a 12-footer can prove beneficial. Fortunately, carbon fibre's inherent 'quick return' is so effective that bites are seldom missed due to the power of the strike failing to reach the hook. Nevertheless, where distances in excess of 60 to 70 yd are involved, and bites are repeatedly missed for no obvious reason, the answer then is to step up to a more powerful

rod (1½ lb or 1¾ lb test curve). Although drastic, such a rod does not bend anywhere near so much on the strike, and therefore pulls more line through the water, setting the hook home firmly. When using a heavier rod, care must really be taken when the tench is almost beaten and is floundering on a short line beneath the rod tip, ready for netting. One last heavy roll on the surface from the fish when you have minimum cushioning in the rod tip might well pull the hook out, or even snap the hook link – so be careful.

When you are ledgering in the conventional way, using either bobbins or monkey climber indicators, and a strong sub-surface tow bellies the line, thus reducing the effectiveness of the strike, you can increase the ratio of bites hit to those missed with a switch to direct or tight-line ledgering using a quiver tip. A quiver tip can be screwed into the tip ring, or you can choose an Avon rod with a built-in quiver tip, the latter being more desirable because it alleviates that 'dead spot' created by the screw-in junction of tip-ring and quiver-tip threads.

The soft glint of early morning sunlight illuminates this matching two-rod set up for catching tench on the feeder from the shallow waters of a large estate lake. Note how high the rods are set above the surface for maximum line pick-up when striking at range.

By cutting the top 20 in from the tip of an Avon blank and sleeving in (from the butt end) approximately the same length of finely tapered, solid-glass donkey top, you can create a wonderful tench tool. An ideal blank is the North Western two-piece, $1\frac{1}{4}$ lb test curve, carbon Kevlar Avon, which is available in both 11 ft and 12 ft versions. Spare top joints can always be obtained for conversion, resulting in an Avon rod with the choice of both standard ledger and quiver tops. Alternatively, consider investing in a ready-made and purposefully designed 'twin top' specialist rod, such as the Ryobi carbon Avon, which is 11 ft long and comprises both standard and quiver tops.

I have purposefully recommended using rods of 11 ft plus because in most circumstances the extra length provides greater control of tench hooked in or just beyond weed and lily-beds. Shorter rods only make extracting the fish more difficult, because the line cannot be held out as far.

REELS

In general terms any small to medium-sized fixed-spool reel, smooth in operation and preferably running on ball bearings, is ideal for tench whether you are float or ledger fishing. Its main requirements are that it must hold at least 100 yd of 3 lb to 7 lb test line depending on the situation at hand, and be equipped with an extremely sensitive slipping clutch which can be tensioned progressively, as opposed to some which appear only to have two settings. Whether it has a stern drag and skirted spool, or has a front-adjusting slipping clutch does not particularly matter. However, as I always play fish with the slipping clutch I insist that the action be smooth in operation. There is nothing more frustrating than snapping up or ripping the hook from a fine tench because the slipping clutch failed to give line when it should have. For many years I used the tiny Mitchell 308 reel (now unobtainable) because of its super-sensitive clutch, when there was little else on the market from which to choose. Nowadays, however, several manufacturers specialize in small reels with super-sensitive slipping clutches. Those made by Shimano, ABU, Ryobi and Shakespeare in the upper price brackets are particularly recommended.

The advantage of choosing a lightweight carbon rod and especially a small, lightweight, compact reel is that a medium-sized species like the tench actually seems that much larger and that much more of an adversary when being played. And quite simply, as a tench is hardly likely to rip off 50 yd of line in long runs, or be fished for at great distances, a large-capacity, large-format reel is not required.

When float fishing at close range only, my preference is for the uncomplicated centre-pin reel, and the two models I use regularly are the match aerial and the Stanton Adcock. The degree of sensitivity and gentle yet progressive drag that can be applied to the rim of the drum on this reel through thumb pressure will always out-do the clutch on any make of fixed-spool or closed-face reel. However, casts of much more than three rod-lengths, especially from overgrown banks, can pose problems to the centre-pin enthusiast. This reel has its limitations too.

LINES

The lines I use for tench fishing range from 2 lb to 6 lb breaking strain, although very occasionally I add a lighter hook length in gin-clear, open-water swims to stimulate bites from really spooky fish. On the other hand, I may also step up to 8 lb test for really big fish in snaggy situations, but this happens very rarely.

Generally speaking I like the control of 3–4 lb test coupled to a match rod when float fishing, and the durability plus safety margin of 6 lb test when ledgering, especially feeder-fishing which is rather risky on anything lighter. Continual distance casting with a heavy feeder puts enormous strain on even the best-quality monofilament line and is foolhardy with anything less than 6 lb test.

Hook lengths of course are invariably lighter, and vary according to the conditions and bait being used at the time. Occasionally I like to use a pre-stretched and consequently much finer hook length when tench are especially shy. A 5 lb-test, pre-stretched mono, for instance, is in diameter little more than a standard 3 lb test, and gives you a great advantage. However, because of the rigours imposed by casting and playing fish, I never use pre-stretched line on the reel.

Tench fishing demands a hard-wearing, abrasion-resistant monofilament line, but also line with a fair degree of elasticity, and for many years I have been satisfied with brands like Sylcast (Sorrel) and Bayer Perlon in mist green. I do, however, follow a simple code. I also change it regularly. The expense is minimal if you purchase line in bulk and keep it stored away from sunlight. Penny-pinching will inevitably cost you lost fish, and terminal rig left on the bottom is a hazard to wildlife.

HOOKS

For virtually all tench fishing requirements, the Drennan chemically-etched, round-bend, straight-eyed, carbon specimen hooks are absolutely ideal. Throughout the entire size range they are relatively light in the wire so as not to overweight the bait, but are forged strongly enough to subdue the biggest tench without springing open.

For those rare occasions when a step down to a light hook link and size 16 or 18 hook is called for, I swap from eyed to the much neater presentation of a spade end hook,

Hooks need to be sharp, forged, and in the smaller sizes exceptionally strong for catching tench. Round-bend, chemically-etched, straight-eyed, carbon specimen hooks are the author's choice.

and choose the Kamasan chemically-etched, round-bend B640 pattern or the Drennan forged-carbon, chub spade-end. Both are strong enough to deal with tench, incredibly sharp, and light enough in the wire to present casters, maggots or very small worms. It you prefer a super-strong, eyed hook for small baits, try the Drennan super-specialist in sizes 16 to 20.

For those occasions when offering whole lobworms, mussel, a duo of cockles, and so on, when a long-shank hook is preferable, the Mustad O'Shaughnessy 34021 pattern in sizes 10 to 6 fits the bill admirably.

As the light begins to fade over a Norfolk lake, the chances of tench moving close in along the fringe of marginal sedges are greatly increased, as this thoughtful fisherman has proved.

KNOTS

For tying all eyed hooks when fishing for tench, there are only two knots you need bother with. The best and most reliable knot is the mahseer knot (fig. 2A). With some patterns of chemically-etched eyed hooks, however, which

FIGURE 2 *Knots*

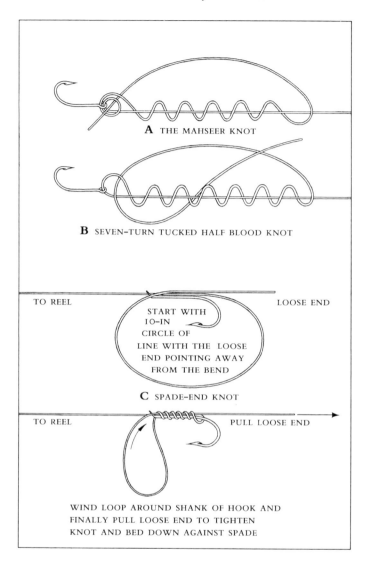

A THE MAHSEER KNOT

B SEVEN-TURN TUCKED HALF BLOOD KNOT

TO REEL   LOOSE END

START WITH
10-IN
CIRCLE OF
LINE WITH THE LOOSE
END POINTING AWAY
FROM THE BEND

C SPADE-END KNOT

TO REEL   PULL LOOSE END

WIND LOOP AROUND SHANK OF HOOK AND
FINALLY PULL LOOSE END TO TIGHTEN
KNOT AND BED DOWN AGAINST SPADE

have a small, extremely neat eye, the end of the line may not pass through twice. In which case I rely on the seven-turn, 'tucked' half blood knot (fig. 2B), which is quick to tie and most reliable. Always remember to wet the line with saliva before pulling the knot gently tight.

For tying spade-end hooks direct to the reel line or to a finer hook length, consider the simple knot in fig. 2C, which requires no threading whatsoever.

To construct a simple fixed paternoster by joining a hook link to the main line, or for adding a ledger or swim-

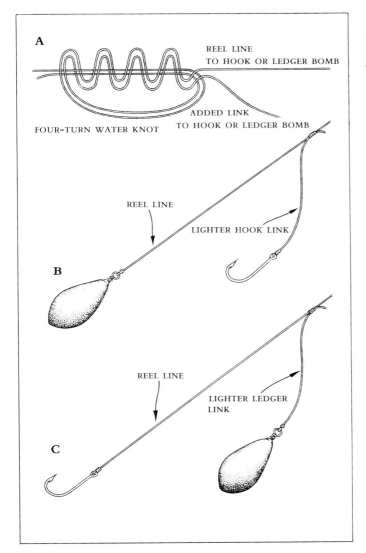

A

REEL LINE
TO HOOK OR LEDGER BOMB

ADDED LINK
FOUR–TURN WATER KNOT   TO HOOK OR LEDGER BOMB

REEL LINE

LIGHTER HOOK LINK

B

REEL LINE

LIGHTER LEDGER
LINK

C

FIGURE 3 *Constructing a simple fixed paternoster*

feeder link which really will stand away from the main line to alleviate tangles, there is nothing to beat the four–turn water knot (fig. 3A). With this simple knot you can safely tie a light hook link to heavier reel line (fig. 3B), or a thick bomb or feeder link (so it doesn't tangle) to a finer reel line (fig. 3C). It is a super knot and particularly neat. It is also good for joining two lines where the only alternative is to use a junction swivel, which can pick up weed rather easily (fig. 4). This problem is alleviated to an extent, however, by the use of a tiny, lightweight, size 12 barrel

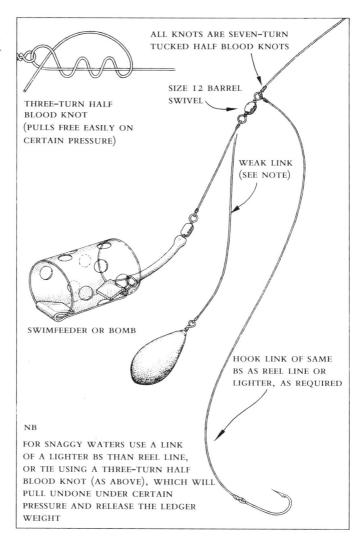

FIGURE 4 *Constructing a fixed paternoster using a barrel swivel*

ALL KNOTS ARE SEVEN–TURN TUCKED HALF BLOOD KNOTS

SIZE 12 BARREL SWIVEL

THREE–TURN HALF BLOOD KNOT (PULLS FREE EASILY ON CERTAIN PRESSURE)

WEAK LINK (SEE NOTE)

SWIMFEEDER OR BOMB

HOOK LINK OF SAME BS AS REEL LINE OR LIGHTER, AS REQUIRED

NB

FOR SNAGGY WATERS USE A LINK OF A LIGHTER BS THAN REEL LINE, OR TIE USING A THREE–TURN HALF BLOOD KNOT (AS ABOVE), WHICH WILL PULL UNDONE UNDER CERTAIN PRESSURE AND RELEASE THE LEDGER WEIGHT

swivel, and by tying both hook link and reel line to one end and the ledger link to the other.

In really overgrown waters where the ledger link may become snagged while trying to extract a big tench from weed-beds, I use a weak link or tie just a three-turn half blood knot, which will pull free at a certain pressure. Thus, using a junction swivel does have its advantages, including the option of being able to change the hook link from long to short or from lighter to heavier quickly without dismantling the entire end rig, using simple seven-turn 'tucked' half blood knots.

INDICATORS

As a direct spin-off from the escalation of 'marketed' carp fishing, many newcomers to tench fishing assume that ledgering the bait in conjunction with an electric alarm offers the best indication of biting fish, which is simply not true. Float fishing is way out ahead in terms of sensitivity and in indicating the most delicate of registrations which tench often give.

Floats

For the lift method all you need is a range of straight, commercial peacock wagglers taking from 1BB up to 1 swan shot. If you can obtain them (try the local zoo or wildlife park) unpainted peacock quills with the herl removed, cut into various lengths from 3 in to 10 in are even better. Simply cover one end in ½ in of matt red or orange fluorescent paint, and attach to the line at the opposite end with a ¼ in section of silicone float rubber. This makes the cheapest, most effective float of all.

Incidentally, you should attach commercial wagglers to the line in the same way if presenting the lift method, *not* with the line threaded through the bottom ring and locked on either side by bulk shot. The lift rig is only effective when the shots are close to the hook.

In addition to straight peacock quill/wagglers, a range of bodied wagglers or drift-beater floats, which have greater shotting capacity, are useful for fishing at distance or in choppy conditions. Not all the mornings when you float-fish for tench will be flat calm and misty.

At the other end of the scale, a range of extremely delicate stillwater antenna floats, possessing extra-fine tips to indicate the merest suggestion of a tench closing its lips over the bait, will also come in handy.

Coil indicators

When freelining large baits such as the insides of a whole medium-sized, freshwater swan mussel, or a couple of lob worms, all you require on the line between butt ring and

reel is a simple coil indicator. These can be made by cutting
1 in diameter plastic piping into 2 in segments, finishing
with a horizontal cut so that each clips easily over the line.
Or by folding two or three layers of silver kitchen foil into
1–2 in wide strips several inches long, and hanging over
the line in a coil. An electric alarm used as the front rod
rest ahead of the coil as an early warning indicator is
optional.

Bobbins

Whether it is used in conjunction with an electric bite
alarm or simply clipped on the line by itself between butt
ring and reel, the basic hair-grip type bobbin is the most
sensitive of all visual indicators. These are obtainable in
dayglo colours, or in clear plastic enclosing luminous
betalight elements, which last for 15 years and suffice for
both daytime and night fishing. Of the various makes
available, the 'Glo Bobbin' is best of all. I have used them
for over 10 years and the betalights still work. However,
the luminosity of betalight elements reduces at somewhere
between 5 to 10 per cent per year. It is a simple matter to
replace them using elements of around 250–300 micro-
lamberts (the strength in which luminosity is rated), which
are quite bright enough to see when you are sitting mere
feet away from the rods.

For connecting the bobbin to the front rod rest do not
use heavy-gauge monofilament, which only twists and
clangs back when the bobbin departs from the line as you
strike. Go for around 2½ ft of old fly line which, due to its
lack of stretch, never tangles and permits the bobbin to
drop harmlessly to the ground on the hardest of strikes. To
the rod-rest end of this retaining line I attach a large
American snap swivel. This easily and quickly clips on to a
tiny ring (the sort used as hook retainers on fly rods)
whipped on to the rod rest (see fig. 5). This process may
sound like a rigmarole, but it is well worth the effort for
convenience sake if you are using bobbin indicators
regularly.

I much prefer clip-on bobbins when ledgering for
species such as bream, roach and tench, as opposed to the
more modern monkey climbers, because I wish to be able

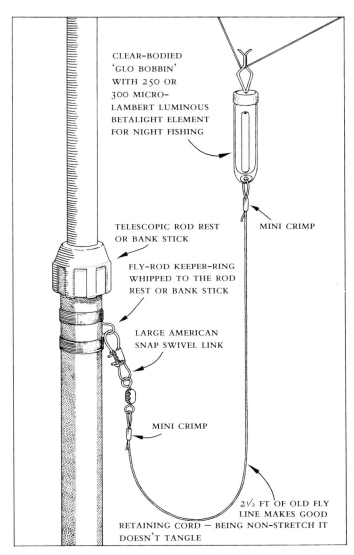

CLEAR-BODIED
'GLO BOBBIN'
WITH 250 OR
300 MICRO-
LAMBERT LUMINOUS
BETALIGHT ELEMENT
FOR NIGHT FISHING

MINI CRIMP

TELESCOPIC ROD REST
OR BANK STICK

FLY-ROD KEEPER-RING
WHIPPED TO THE ROD
REST OR BANK STICK

LARGE AMERICAN
SNAP SWIVEL LINK

MINI CRIMP

2½ FT OF OLD FLY
LINE MAKES GOOD
RETAINING CORD — BEING NON-STRETCH IT
DOESN'T TANGLE

FIGURE 5 *Bobbin indicator set-up*

to see the very tiniest indication of a bite. With a bobbin
clipped on to the line between butt ring and reel this
happens, provided it hangs vertically down immediately
below the butt ring. If a fish moves the bait 6 in the bobbin
will rise 6 in, as in fig. 6A. If it is suspended midway
between butt ring and reel (fig. 6B) it will register a
reduced bite. This is because the line slides through the
bobbin clip as the bobbin moves, the bobbin can only rise
half that distance – just 3 in.

This is exactly what happens when a monkey climber

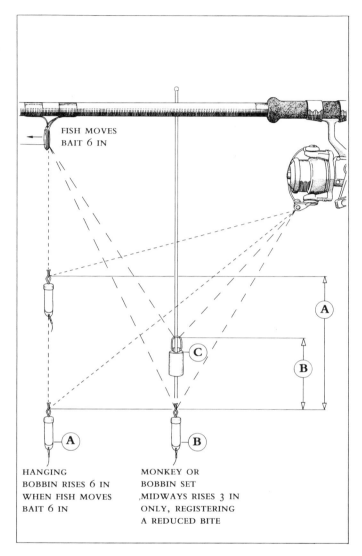

FISH MOVES BAIT 6 IN

A

B

C

A

B

HANGING BOBBIN RISES 6 IN WHEN FISH MOVES BAIT 6 IN

MONKEY OR BOBBIN SET MIDWAYS RISES 3 IN ONLY, REGISTERING A REDUCED BITE

indicator is positioned where it operates at its smoothest – midway between butt ring and reel (fig. 6C) – giving a reduced bite indication every time, equal to only half the distance the fish moved the bait. When tench provide positive bite indications, this is perhaps not so worrying, but there are times when I expect to hit mere ¼ in movements of the bobbin, whether up or down. After all, if a float with ¼ in of its tip visible above the surface suddenly vanished, it would be considered a good bite. Ledgering indicators should work on the same basis.

A sensibly arranged two-rod set-up using ledger bobbins in conjunction with Optonic bite indicators. The ideal combination for attacking distant swims when float-fishing is impractical.

To counteract wind drift or a strong underwater tow which slowly pulls the line and raises the bobbin, simply pinch one, two or even three swan shot on the retaining cord immediately below the bobbin.

Monkey climbers

When used in the best position for the monkey to rise freely (i.e., suspended midway between butt ring and reel) this indicator can only move half the distance the bait has been pulled by the tench. When fishing in gale force winds, however, because the indicator is held on a needle and does not swing about (like a bobbin), the monkey climber has an advantage over other methods.

The 'grease monkies' manufactured by Gardner Tackle, with black, PTFE-coated, stainless steel needles and segmented bodies which can be made 'lighter' or 'heavier', are really excellent. There is a vertical hole in the main body for the insertion of a betalight for night fishing.

BITE ALARMS/BUZZERS

Whether freelining and using a silver foil indicator or ledgering with a bobbin set up, reliance on the piercing call of an antenna or optonic type buzzer to jar the brain into immediate action certainly puts a lot more tench on the bank. Bite alarms allow you, with the help of binoculars, to capitalize on what's happening in other parts of the fishery where the tench are moving, or to relax and delight in the sights and sounds of the natural history. At a moment's notice, it's possible to turn around and instantly focus your attention – and striking arm – on the indicator (if using a two-rod set up), which rises or falls as the alarm shrieks its warning.

Optonic bite indicators

I can relate to this particular alarm, which is also a bite indicator, more easily than all others. For every $\frac{1}{4}$ in of line which travels across the sensitive, frictionless wheel, a single bleep tone plus warning light is emitted, which means that instantly I know whether the bite is a mere twitch, a slow run, or a fast run – and can react accordingly. For example if there are numerous tench in a confined, shallow weedy area and the bobbin 'jingles' every so often because a fish bumps into the line registering a single bleep I gear my mind to ignore these 'liners' and respond only to more positive indications. On other occasions, however, when bites are few and far between, I may strike instantly at a single bleep identifying it as a diminutive bite, especially if, having ignored previous single bleeps, I have reeled in afterwards to find that the maggots or corn have been sucked to skins.

The Optonic works only when the line moves forwards

or backwards (as in a drop-back bite). The moving line rotates a tiny fan-blade on the wheel spindle, either side of which is a photo-electric cell. When the indicator is switched on these two cells are connected by an invisible beam of light. Whenever the light beam is interrupted by the fan, the indicator bleeps. It is so simple yet devastatingly effective, and is available in various self-contained, cord-less compact models, with or without volume and tone control. In some models the sensor heads are connected by wires to a sounder box, which can be positioned several yards away. It was on a tench fishing trip that I reviewed the Optonic indicator when it first became available and took the tackle trade by storm in 1978. I caught a fair bag of tench that day under difficult conditions too, many of them due to the indicator's effectiveness and I have forgotten how many hundreds of tench it has accounted for since.

The only drawback, and some might say it creates an unacceptable disturbance to the peacefulness and tranquillity of beautiful tench lakes and pits, is that a large proportion of anglers will insist on informing every other angler about the number of bites they are having by turning the Optonic's volume control up far too loudly.

I am often asked why it is that I rarely use buzzer bars which allow for two (or more) Optonics to be neatly assembled on a single telescopic bankstick or butt rest. I like to have the option of being able, within seconds, to angle one rod in a completely different direction to the other (something which is not possible with buzzer-bar set-ups); for example, to cover a tench which has just rolled or to place a bait over rising bubbles, both of which could happen well away from the baited area. The back rests are not disturbed; I simply pull the front one out and reposition it so the rod is in a direct line with the point where the bait is to be cast. It means carrying four telescopic bank sticks about instead of two, or course, but to my opportunist mind it is well worth the effort.

Incidentally, if you intend doing a fair amount of ledgering for tench using bite indicators, it is well worth investing in good-quality bank sticks with solid points for working easily into hard gravel and sensible locking collars for quick height adjustment. Those made of stainless steel are particularly recommended.

The audible indication of a bite alarm allows you to relax while ledgering for tench in large open waters, and to capitalize on what is happening in other areas. Search the surface with bin-oculars for signs of the tench's presence, and you may catch bonus fish.

SUNDRIES

Landing-nets

As few tench exceed a length of 24 in, a landing-net of that size with either a triangular or round frame is more than adequate. Size for size, my preference will always be for the round frame, because it provides more netting area (fig. 7).

I also like a deep 24 in twin-mesh net which has minnow-mesh sides and a flat, micromesh bottom upon which the tench gently rests for unhooking without small shots or bombs slipping through and tangling. Weighing a shade over 1lb when wet, this net is also tailor-made for weighing the tench without going to all the bother of wetting a specialized weigh sling and moving the fish from one to the other. You simply unscrew the landing-net pole and hoist net frame plus tench onto the scales, remembering to deduct the net frame afterwards. To permit netting of tench caught around reed stems or amongst lilies well out

For netting tench of all sizes, a round, 24 in diameter frame fitted with a deep, twin-mesh net screwed into a long, telescopic fibreglass handle is perfect.

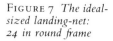

FIGURE 7 *The ideal-sized landing-net: 24 in round frame*

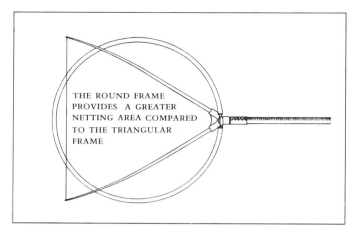

THE ROUND FRAME PROVIDES A GREATER NETTING AREA COMPARED TO THE TRIANGULAR FRAME

from the bank, I use the longest telescopic glass landing-net pole that I can comfortably wield.

Keep-nets/sacks

Having used both soft nylon sacks and micro-meshed keep-nets for well over a decade, I am still undecided as to which is more suitable for the purpose and less harmful to the fish. I suspect that both are tench friendly, and that being dark and soft the fish lie quiet inside, without having their protective layer of body mucus removed. And so, depending on convenience, I shall continue to use both and recommend the reader enjoys the same choice.

The main point to consider is that wet keep-nets are heavy to carry at the end of a session. If you have a long walk from the car when fishing a lake that rarely produces more than one or two tench per session, then the easily portable sack is the obvious choice. If you are parked close to a swim where a big bag of tench is on the cards, a large micro-mesh net somewhere between 10 and 12 ft long and with a 20 in diameter is the best choice.

Unhooking mats

The foam-lined unhooking mats used for carp fishing, which protect the fish whenever the banks are unfriendly as many gravel pit fisheries are, work wonderfully well with tench. If you purchase a large mat at the outset, it will suffice for carp, pike, and medium-sized species such as bream and tench. Do not, however, take the tench out of the landing-net and lie it on the unhooking mat. Simply lower the net on to the mat and use the wet mesh for holding the tench in your left hand while unhooking it with your right. The tench can then be lowered straight back into the water, or in to the top of the keep net, and the landing-net reversed to free the fish with the minimum of handling.

Weed rakes/drags

If you are committed, either through lack of transport or local choice, to tench fishing in extremely weedy fisheries, some sort of weed-clearing device is essential if you wish to continue fishing throughout the summer.

Rakes or drags designed specifically for the angler are not manufactured, but it is not difficult to make your own. For years tench fishermen have been wiring together (use 20 gauge galvanized wire) the steel heads of two garden rakes back to back, and tying on a long length of

FIGURE 8 *Home-made weed rake*

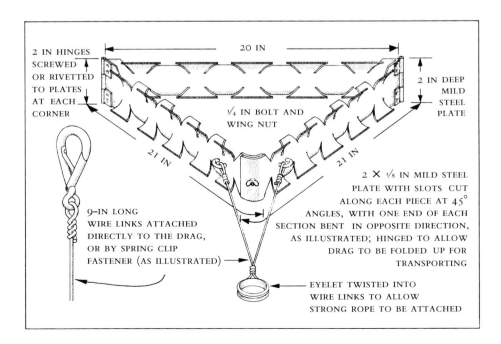

2 IN HINGES SCREWED OR RIVETTED TO PLATES AT EACH CORNER

20 IN

2 IN DEEP MILD STEEL PLATE

¼ IN BOLT AND WING NUT

21 IN

21 IN

9-IN LONG WIRE LINKS ATTACHED DIRECTLY TO THE DRAG, OR BY SPRING CLIP FASTENER (AS ILLUSTRATED)

2 × ⅛ IN MILD STEEL PLATE WITH SLOTS CUT ALONG EACH PIECE AT 45° ANGLES, WITH ONE END OF EACH SECTION BENT IN OPPOSITE DIRECTION, AS ILLUSTRATED; HINGED TO ALLOW DRAG TO BE FOLDED UP FOR TRANSPORTING

EYELET TWISTED INTO WIRE LINKS TO ALLOW STRONG ROPE TO BE ATTACHED

'throwing' rope securely in the middle. This makes a cheap and most efficient tool for pulling out dense lilies or other surface plants and for removing rampant soft weeds such as Canadian pond weed or mill foil.

During the winter months there is no better time for constructing your own designer weed drag. An excellent pattern (fig. 8) handed down to me by my old friend Bill Cooper of Norwich has, over the years, proved to be most useful. It is light, well worth the trouble to make, and really cleans out a swim fast, whatever it happens to be clogged with.

Alternatively, it's well worth scanning the tool section at your local garden centre, where a range of interesting and useful rakes and rake heads of every conceivable description are available at a price.

CHAPTER FIVE

BAITS

IF my tench fishing was limited to the use of just one bait, I would find it difficult to choose between bread flake, worms and sweetcorn. Fortunately there is no such restriction, and I can enjoy using and experimenting with a whole variety of baits to suit the situation at hand, from the humble shop-bought maggot to designer milk protein pastes. In recent years, tench which previously only saw the more conventional, commonly-used baits at the start of each new season, are now bombarded with every carp bait ever invented. And once they have learnt to accept baits such as boilies and the popular particles like peanuts or black-eyed beans as natural food, because they are so regularly introduced into the water, tench acquire a genuine taste for them.

Wherever tench share a fishery with carp, it is as well to accept that if any amount of pre-baiting has taken place with particles or boilies, then these baits could indeed outfish the old standbys like maggots, worms and corn. So don't bang your head against a brick wall. If the tench want boilies, let them have boilies. Tench also respond well to attractor baits such as tares and hempseed, which again were probably used initially to attract carp into the margins, but which eventually draw more and more tench into the area.

Tench are noticeably attracted by all mass baits such as corn, casters and maggots, because their natural staple diet of bloodworms (midge larvae) abounds in the silt by the million. They are therefore not so alarmed by them as they might be by the sight of a large piece of bread flake sitting on the bottom. Although perhaps this is unfair, because bread is one of the most effective baits for tench.

At the end of the day there is no best bait for tench, or indeed for any fish. It is a case of trial and error. So let us explore the tench fisherman's potential armoury, starting with naturals, where fishing baits first began, with worms and the garden fork.

NATURALS

Worms

Few other baits are treated with the same aggression or instigate such positive bites as worms. I rate lobworms extremely highly as a specimen tench bait whatever the conditions, and especially during windy weather and in low water temperatures when tench generally are not responding.

To make a large ledgered lobworm gyrate attractively several inches above the bottom weed, inject a little air into the head with a hypodermic syringe. Be very careful when doing this, however, because if the needle slips and you accidentally inject air into your finger, the result could be fatal. Lobworm sections threaded up the shank and topped with a couple of maggots or a single grain of corn work well, too.

You should never set off tench fishing without brandlings, those yellow-banded wrigglers found in manure heaps. Few naturals have such instant pulling power as brandlings presented two or three up on a size 12 or 10 hook, topped with a single maggot so they cannot wriggle off over the barb. Whenever there is enough to go round, catapult a few fragments of chopped worms, lobs or brandlings, into the swim around the float, or mix them into the groundbait for throwing or catapulting out while ledgering.

Mussels

Next to the bloodworm, there cannot be a more natural bait to offer the tench than the freshwater swan mussel. Nearly every stillwater and even fast-flowing rivers abound with this mollusc, which always grows to its largest (often exceeding 6 in in length) in the mineral richness of the siltiest lakes and pits. They live with their shell part-buried in the detritus, feeding and breathing by continually syphoning water through their system. They do in fact move rather more quickly than one would imagine, with a keel-like foot protruding from the bottom corner of their blunt end. In thick silt they leave behind a definite furrow.

Gather mussels by pulling a long-handled garden rake along the bottom through the margins. Some areas will be far more prolific than others, so don't despair if you are not immediately successful. In really muddy or silty shallows, it's just as easy to roll your sleeves up and feel for them. They can easily be kept alive for several days in a bucket of water, but soon die and go off when left dry.

To open the clam-like shell do not try and prize it apart with your fingers. It fractures surprisingly easy, and the jagged edges are capable of inflicting a nasty wound. Enter the shell with a thin-bladed knife and sever the powerful hinges at each end, whereupon it will open readily. Tench adore the large, orange-coloured, meaty insides, whether presented whole on a size 4, or chopped into smaller chunks. Many a tench angler has struck a confident run on whole mussel, only to find that a specimen rudd or roach was the greedy culprit. Do not worry about what appears to be an oversize bait; it easily folds and gets sucked in by those rubbery lips. Whole mussels are best freelined (p. 85), resulting in the most positive runs you are ever likely to encounter from a tench. Pre-bait for a few days, scattering the chopped-up insides of, say, a dozen mussels into a favourite known tench swim. Then try one on the hook.

Cockles

Whether tench respond eagerly to cockles because the orange meat reminds them of a baby swan mussel, I cannot say. However, following a few days of pre-baiting, cockles will have tench climbing up the rod – or they will produce absolutely no interest at all.

Buy them in bulk ready-boiled from the fishmongers, and separate into smaller batches in polybags before popping into the freezer for later use. Prior to freezing, they can be coloured with the same powder dye used in making carp baits. Simply add a teaspoonful of dye to half a cupful of hot water and pour over the cockles in a 2 pt bait tin. Colour the cockles in 1 pt batches, stirring gently until they are evenly coloured, then strain off excess dye before freezing.

Tench have a distinct preference for the smell of natural baits. Worms, especially brandlings, are at the top of the list.

Tench love the aroma of natural baits. When you find it impossible to collect a fresh batch of lobworms from the lawn after dark, both prawns and cockles are worth trying instead.

Prawns and shrimps

Again, these are most cheaply bought in bulk (several pints at a time) from the fishmongers ready boiled and peeled. Split them into separate batches for freezing. As with cockles, pre-baiting over a period of several days will allow the tench to acquire a liking for the succulent meat, which is best presented beneath a float lift style (p. 88). Long casting is rather risky as the soft meat tears easily and will fly off in mid air.

Maggots

These are a fine tench bait, though being the most commonly-used bait of all, their effectiveness quickly wears off once tench start to become suspicious of them. It is then a case of reducing both hook and line size until tench feel confident in sucking the maggot or maggots in, which is not really a satisfactory situation in heavily weeded waters. So whilst they are among the first choice in baits with which to commence the new season, don't prolong their use when bites slow up.

Maggots that have been dyed red seem to have the edge, perhaps because they then become associated with blood-worm by the tench.

Casters

These are rated by many keen tench fishermen as a more productive bait than maggots. Certainly their presence in groundbait really gets the tench rooting about, especially if all the juices are squeezed out of the casters and mixed into the groundbait. It seems to add that extra inexplicable 'something'.

Casters are great presented singly on a size 16, or two and three up on a size 14 or 12. However, they are even more effective in a 'cocktail' with sweetcorn, brandlings or red maggots. When fishing over heavy bottom-weed, two dark (buoyant) casters will suspend a size 14 hook nicely just on top of the weed.

PARTICLE BAITS

Sweetcorn

Of all the particle baits that attract tench, sweetcorn is by far the most effective, whether ledgered or float-fished. One piece on a size 14 is about right, or three up on a size 12 or 10. It all depends on the size of the kernels. Tinned sweetcorn tends to be noticeably smaller (and more expensive) than the frozen variety.

For presenting a really good mouthful when tench are spitting out the skins without registering a bite, simply thread two or three kernels up and over the eye of a size 8 hook onto the line above. Then slip three kernels on to the hook and slide the others gently back down again. It works wonders.

On heavily fished waters, sweetcorn's effectiveness is reduced because everyone tends to rely on its pulling power, particularly early in the season. In this case, terminal tackle must be scaled down if you wish to stay catching on corn. It is not that the tench stop eating it; far from it, all the loose feed certainly gets mopped up. They simply become suspicious of corn on the hook. You then have three choices. Rig up a short hair and present it off the hook. Change its colour from yellow to red or orange (using a powder carp bait dye), or stop using it and change to another bait.

Stewed wheat

This is easy to prepare, and is a great follow-on or alternative particle to sweetcorn. Put a few pints into a plastic bucket with a rip-off lid, cover by at least several inches of boiling water (to allow the grains to expand fully), and push the lid on firmly. Within a few hours the excess water can be strained off, and the succulent kernels, with their distinct 'nutty' aroma, can be separated into batches and popped into the freezer for later use.

You can dye stewed wheat red, purple or orange by adding powder dye to the boiling water. Give this bait a good try. Tench love it, and you can purchase a sack of wheat for a few pounds.

Hempseed and tares

Although tench are caught with these particles presented on the hook, I think of them more as attractor baits, to be scattered or catapulted either as loose feed or mixed into the groundbait, whilst using other 'larger' baits on the hook. Prepare them overnight in boiling water as for stewed wheat, and then leave for a couple of days for the seeds to ferment in their own juices. Don't worry about the smell, tench love it.

Beans, peas and nuts

Beans such as haricots, black eyed beans, red kidney beans, chickpeas and peanuts do not have the 'instant' tench appeal of maggots, worms, bread or sweetcorn. However, they are all effective particle baits in fisheries where they have been exhaustively used to attract carp, and where eventually the tench have also learnt to accept them as food. For 'carp-orientated' tench, black-eyes and peanuts especially seem to be favoured. They may be float-fished lift style (p. 88), on or off a hair, and ledgered bolt-style (p. 121) either side-hooked or on a hair. The permutations on any particular water are as endless as for carp fishing.

Boilies

As I have already mentioned, boilies are very popular with tench in fisheries which have been heavily pre-baited to attract carp. By the same token, after several pre-baiting sessions boilies will also catch tench on waters where carp do not exist, but where most standard tench baits like worms, paste, maggots, and soft particles are ripped to pieces by hoards of small nuisance fish such as perch, roach or rudd.

Once the tench (like carp) become suspicious of the standard, side-hooked boilie (fig. 9A), thread them off the hook on to a fine hair (fig. 9B). This gives the tench greater confidence when sucking them up, and conse-quently produces more bites. Shock or bolt rig tactics are

Probably the most instant tench bait ever used, sweetcorn can be offered in a good mouthful by threading three kernels onto the line and sliding them up against another three on the hook.

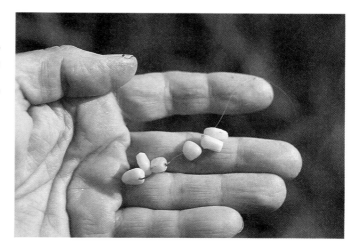

Be forever willing to experiment by varying bait combinations when bites are not forthcoming. A cocktail of sweetcorn that has been dyed red and maggots led to the downfall of this lovely fish.

not necessarily required. Boilies work well presented in the lift style beneath a buoyant peacock quill (see Lift method, p. 88), and on a standard feeder rig (see 'Ledgering' p. 108). When these and all other avenues fail to produce hittable bites, the time has arrived to present the boilie bolt-style. Most respectably-sized tench can easily manage 14 mm to 18 mm boilies, but they do show a marked preference for 8 mm to 10 mm mini boilies. The yellow minis produced by Richworth (Honey Yukatan), probably owing to their colour and similarity in size to sweetcorn, are worth trying first. You can then ring the changes through the difficult colours and flavours, moving on to larger boilies as the situation dictates.

A comprehensive selection of baits suitable for a day's feeder fishing – hook offerings of red and yellow sweetcorn, brandlings, bread, casters, maggots and boilies, plus slightly dampened bread crumbs for plugging each end of the feeder.

Best colours overall seem to be yellow, red and orange, while either very sweet or seafood flavours are the best attractors. Try pre-baiting with mini boilies but using a 14 mm one on the hook so it really stands out. Or pre-bait with tares or hempseed and fish a mini boilie on the hook. There are countless permutations with which to experiment.

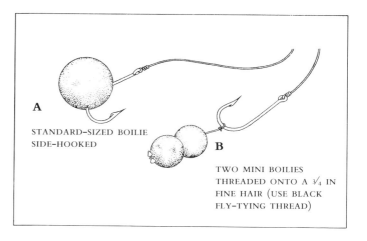

A

STANDARD–SIZED BOILIE
SIDE–HOOKED

B

TWO MINI BOILIES
THREADED ONTO A ¾ IN
FINE HAIR (USE BLACK
FLY–TYING THREAD)

PASTES

Soft protein pastes

The same milk-based protein ingredients as are used in boiled baits, mixed with water, flavouring and colouring, make exceptionally fine paste baits for tench. If you like to make your own boilies give yourself a treat and save yourself time by using your favourite recipe as a soft paste, just as it is prior to being rolled into balls and boiled. The main reason for boiling is to produce a protective skin around the bait which irritating, unwanted species cannot pick at (boilies were first created for carp, remember). So if your tench lake is not rampant with shoals of paste-nicking shoal fish, allow the tench to sample large soft paste baits either float-fished, freelined or ledgered.

A piece of paste the size of a 50 p coin, covering a size 6 hook and flattened so it flutters slowly down and settles gently on top of any soft weed, is absolutely ideal. To pre-bait, introduce a few dozen paste pieces into several adjoining swims (so all the local tench see them) every other day over a period of a week or two. Then start using them on the hook. You could be amazed at the pulling power of soft paste. To make the paste really buoyant, so it rests ever so gently on top of weed, use a couple of ounces of sodium casenate in the base mix. A good formula to start with is equal proportions (say 4 oz each) of calcium casenate, wheatgerm, lactopro and soya isolate, plus water and your choice of flavour and powder colouring, all kneaded together to produce a soft but slightly rubbery texture. Tench do tend to shy away from white (un-coloured) pastes – possibly it reminds them too much of white bread flake, on which they may have been repeatedly caught in the past.

Trout pellet paste

This evil-smelling khaki-coloured paste, a concoction of fish meals and grains, will really get tench going. It is available in pellet form, and you can either break it down to dust in a coffee-grinder (a handful at a time), then add warm water and knead into a paste, adding wheat gluten or cornflour to bind; or dampen the pellets liberally with hot water and wait an hour or so before kneading and adding the binders.

A favourite old carp recipe which tench adore is to add a spoonful or two of phillips yeast mixture (a bird tonic available from pet shops) to the pellet paste.

Trout pellet paste is best freelined or ledgered, but like all baits can be presented beneath a float. For loose feed, scatter in some pellet mash (to which extra water has been added so it clouds the swim) around your hook bait. When using pellet mash, you will need an old towel for wiping your hands.

Bread paste

Bread paste is considered rather old hat, but its creamy consistency will attract tench from a great many waters. For the best paste you need old bread. Give it a good soaking, and squeeze out all the excess water; then knead it thoroughly into a firm yet pliable paste.

It can be coloured (use powder dye), and it may be flavoured with liquid essences. It fact, all sorts of additives can be included. Finely grated cheddar cheese used 50/50 with bread paste, plus a spoonful of marmite, makes a fabulous tangy bait; it can be fozen and used at any time. Alternatively, try sausage-meat, again used 50/50 with bread paste, with additives like marmite, bovril or a crushed oxo cube kneaded in.

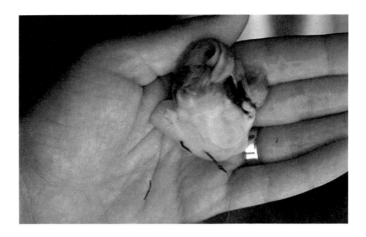

The orange insides of a freshwater swan mussel, which abound in the mud or among the gravel shallows of most lakes and pits, make a fine natural bait for tench. Freeline on a size 4 hook tied direct to 5 or 6 lb line.

Sausagemeat

This is a very effective bait, especially in heavily-coloured waters. It can be used just as it is with a little cornflour added to stiffen it into a paste.

Cooked sausages also tempt tench. Any type – pork, beef, spicy, or frankfurthers straight from the tin – can be cut into ½ in cubes, which suffices for both loose feed and hook baits. And I dare you to go tench fishing with a bag of sausage cubes without eating a few.

Tinned meats like that good old standby, luncheon meat (always carry a tin in the tackle bag), may be cut into oblongs or cubes of any size. For particularly spooky tench they are best presented on a fine hair rig.

Luncheon meat

No tackle bag or car boot should ever be without a tin of luncheon meat or two. This bait should be standard issue to every young angler with his first rod and reel outfit. Don't be fussy about brands. Simply cube the meat with a long-bladed, very sharp knife, ensuring that the cubes measure exactly the length of the hook. That way,

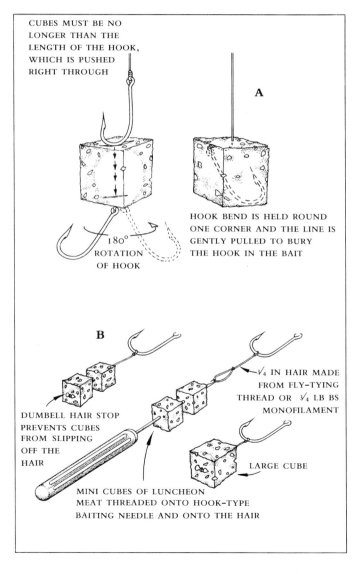

CUBES MUST BE NO LONGER THAN THE LENGTH OF THE HOOK, WHICH IS PUSHED RIGHT THROUGH

A

180° ROTATION OF HOOK

HOOK BEND IS HELD ROUND ONE CORNER AND THE LINE IS GENTLY PULLED TO BURY THE HOOK IN THE BAIT

B

DUMBELL HAIR STOP PREVENTS CUBES FROM SLIPPING OFF THE HAIR

¼ IN HAIR MADE FROM FLY-TYING THREAD OR ¼ LB BS MONOFILAMENT

LARGE CUBE

MINI CUBES OF LUNCHEON MEAT THREADED ONTO HOOK-TYPE BAITING NEEDLE AND ONTO THE HAIR

FIGURE 10A
Hooking on luncheon meat and B hair-rigged luncheon meat cubes

hooking on meat will never pose a problem. Simply push the hook through the middle of the cube (fig. 10A) until you can grip the bend with your fingernails, and pull through. Then push the point and bend around a corner and gently pull on the line. The hook will be completely hidden, yet will cut through the meat immediately on the strike. Luncheon meat cubes (and sausage cubes) can, of course, also be threaded on to a hair, using a couple of mini cubes or one large one (fig. 10B).

BREAD

Last but not least, don't forget the pulling power of good, old-fashioned breadflake. Used in large lumps on size 6 or 8 hooks, breadflake has the uncanny knack of producing the larger tench. It is also effective, for finicky fish, presented on much smaller hooks, as is a small cube of breadcrust. Crust is very effective in swims that are heavily carpeted in soft weed; its inherent buoyancy means that it is always visible. A small piece of crust threaded up the shank of a size 10 hook with a couple of casters or maggots on the bend makes an electric cocktail. All sorts of combinations are worth persevering with (fig. 11).

FIGURE 11
Combinations and cocktails when using bread

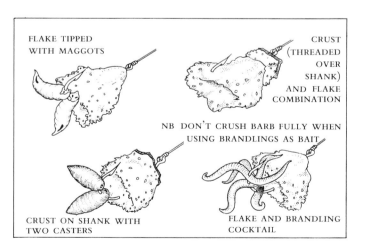

FLAKE TIPPED WITH MAGGOTS

CRUST (THREADED OVER SHANK) AND FLAKE COMBINATION

NB DON'T CRUSH BARB FULLY WHEN USING BRANDLINGS AS BAIT

CRUST ON SHANK WITH TWO CASTERS

FLAKE AND BRANDLING COCKTAIL

GROUNDBAITS

In certain situations, such as fishing waters low in stocks of tench but where individual fish run to specimen proportions, groundbaiting – other than scattering out a few hook bait fragments – is not required. Indeed, it might have the reverse effect and actually scare off a handful of wily old tench from approaching the swim. On the other hand, where tench are present in abundant numbers and need to be weaned away from their daily diet of aquatic insects, shrimps, bloodworms and the like, a liberal helping of groundbait, incorporating hook-bait fragments, is very much the order of the day.

For the groundbait base there is nothing to beat plain brown breadcrumbs. If it is going to be packed into an open-ended feeder, the crumbs need to be coarse so that they create an exploding effect when they suddenly swell on absorbing water. If the groundbait is going to be thrown or catapulted, the crumbs can be coarse or fine.

To the plain crumb, add a few cupfuls each of maize meal (to give that 'sweetcorn' appeal), salmon fry crumbs or ground trout pellets, hempseed or boiled rice, plus fragments of the hook-bait such as casters, maggots, chopped worms, sweetcorn or chopped mini boilies. A spoonful or two (per bucket) of yellow or orange powder dye helps to cloud water which is on the clear side.

I have been known to mix this up two or three days prior to using it, to give the natural yeasts time to start fermenting. Tench adore the smell, but you would be well advised not to squeeze out the balls ready for throwing in the early morning if you have a hangover.

PRE-BAITING, DRAGGING AND RAKING

Whenever time permits I like to pre-bait new areas or new fisheries at least a night or two before the first early-morning fishing session. If tench in good numbers are known to be there, then half a bucket of groundbait is a

Swims that are completely choked with surface plants such as the dwarf pond lily and therefore unfishable can, with the help of a weed rake or drag, quickly be transformed into ideal float-fishing spots.

good measure to start with. More can always be introduced during the session if the tench continue to feed well into daylight following the magical dawn-feeding period. A small quantity of fresh blood (obtainable from a butcher) mixed into the groundbait provides added attraction for the fish, especially after the swim has been raked or dragged.

Opinions vary as to when is the best time to drag a tench swim; or if to drag it at all. Some say the evening is best before a dawn start, some say immediately prior to fishing. Having taken good hauls after dragging at both times, I am not really fussy. However, I would perhaps bend towards the latter view on the grounds that I won't have missed any tench attracted to the area during the night which have subsequently departed, bellies full of free feed.

It is necessary to understand what is achieved by raking out a clear patch of water amongst dense weed, apart from allowing the fish to move about more freely, because the effect can prove three-fold.

Firstly, the sound waves attract tench (the most curious of fishes) to the area like bees to a honey-pot. Secondly, they have a nice surprise when they arrive because all the tiny, single items of food which they normally have to grub about to find are conveniently presented – along with your loose feed. Lastly, the thick cloud of silt which might be held in suspension for up to several hours depending upon water temperature and the number of tench which arrive in the swim and keep it churned up, makes them feel more secure.

If you own a pair of chest-waders, and your favourite tench lake is neither too deep nor too silty, take along a long-handled garden rake and give the bottom, whether weedy or not, a good raking. I wish I had a fiver for every time during high summer that I have stripped down to my underpants and got in to clear a swim of its weeds, or simply to churn the bottom up. Neighbouring anglers might hand out a few old-fashioned looks, but their faces soon change when they see your rod bending a few minutes later. And don't be afraid to get out there and give the bottom a good going over at any time of the day, especially when the sun is well up, sport has stopped and the tench have retreated into the thickest weed. It cannot do anything but improve your chances.

CHAPTER SIX

TECHNIQUES AND RIGS

FREELINING

Freelining is exactly what the term implies: nothing is attached to the line that could impair natural presentation, only the hook and bait. The line is free of all shots, floats and ledger rigs. This is why the technique produces such confident bites from tench in clear waters which, through suspicion, might otherwise dither or play about with the bait, especially float-fished baits where the line is vertical from shots to float as in the lift method.

Large baits heavy enough in themselves to disguise the hook and neutralize its weight, such as the insides of a whole swan mussel, a lump of trout pellet paste or a lobworm, are each also heavy enough to cast accurately from a well-filled spool without added weight. Freelining is therefore a method which can only be practised at close range where tench are attracted to natural habitats: gaps between beds of marginal sedges, rushes or reeds; alongside and even into beds of lily pads; beneath the overhanging branches of willow or alder; and beside trees whose lower limbs are part sunken.

Some of the most exciting tench I have caught while freelining came during the heat of the afternoon from beneath a canopy of partly submerged rhododendrons. These particular tench live in a beautiful, secluded mere and invariably disappeared from all the popular swims once the sun rose high in the sky. Even from my spying tree, an old cedar whose branches reached out a good 30 ft above the surface, I could see nothing through the crystal-clear water, which was nowhere deeper than 4 ft, save for shoals of immature rudd and countless mussel shells. It was so clear that even those spots where the resident heron liked to fish could be pinpointed by the preponderance of open mussel shells close in to the bank.

It was a phenomenon which always had me puzzled until one afternoon when, completely by accident, whilst peering into the water through polaroid glasses I happened to notice a pair of black tails protruding from beneath the maze of partly-sunken rhododendron branches hanging way out over the margins.

Despite a depth of just 18 in, there were days when it seemed as though the mere's entire population of tench would take refuge in the shade of just two albeit large rhododendrons. The attraction was two-fold: subdued light in a mere barren of lilies, combined with a readily available food source of aquatic insect larvae clinging to the sunken woodwork.

I would flip a fat lobworm hooked once only through the head by a size 6 hook, tied direct to 6 lb line (the beauty of freelining is that it permits the use of sensible tackle), into the gaps between the branches and allow it to reach bottom. If there was no response after a minute or so I twitched it back slowly, pausing every so often in case it had been sighted.

A slamming take more reminiscent of weed-raft chub than tench could happen at any moment. A large lump of

Opposite: Using the tall stems of yellow iris as cover, John kneels low to freeline a whole lobworm to tench working the warm marginal shallows.

A bunch of maggots, fished tight up to a bed of sweet reed grass beneath a waggler in just 3 ft of water, accounted for this plump 5 lb gravel-pit tench.

FIGURE 12
(Opposite) *The mechanics of the lift method*

breadflake was always a good substitute when the lob-worms ran out, or were unobtainable, and the meaty insides of a swan mussel also produced results. Unfortunately, a higher ratio of eels to tench than was desirable invariably came to mussel, so the gyrating lobworm was always favourite.

Anglers who have only ever float-fished for tench, using light float tackle in heavily fished waters and straining their eyes for those tiny dips or lifts of the float tip in order to strike, would not believe the way in which tench run off with a freelined bait. But then, with an unweighted bait they have no reason to be fussy. They simply suck it in and move off looking for the next meal, lifting the line in a glorious, unmissable, almost carp-like run.

If immediate bites are expected, do not bother with indicators. Hold the rod and keep your eyes glued to the bow in the line from rod tip to surface. If not, hang a lightweight foil indicator on a 2 ft drop between butt ring and reel, after positioning the rod on two rests with the tip pointing directly at the bait. Whack the hook home just before the indicator slams against the butt ring.

With minimal resistance on the line, the tench is just as likely to swim towards the rod and give a 'drop back', whereupon the indicator suddenly falls to the ground. This is a good reason for always keeping the bale arm closed when freelining, enabling you to go straight into a 'wind-cum-strike' routine in order to pick up the line and punch the hook home.

When freelining into darkness or when tench activity is on the slow side, rig up an electric alarm in conjunction with the foil indicator so you can relax. You can certainly afford to, because bites are nearly always positive.

FLOAT FISHING

The lift method

No other float-fishing technique has been so exhaustively described as the famous lift method. Yet even now, almost 40 years since the Taylor brothers first popularized the method back in the 1950s with their huge catches of

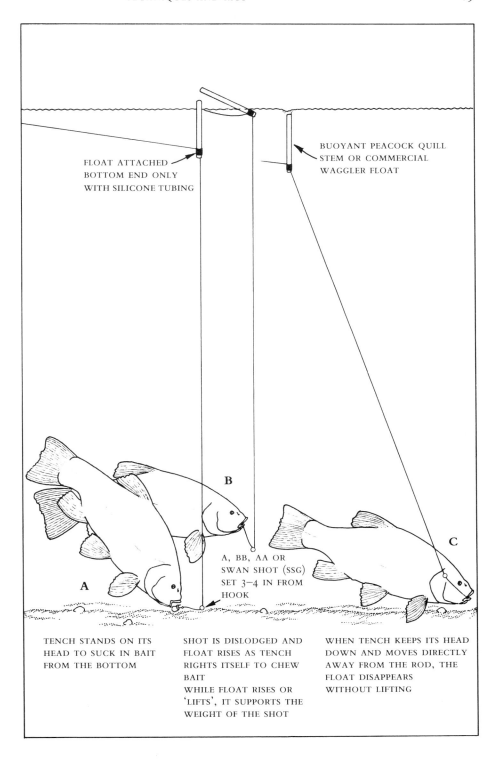

FLOAT ATTACHED
BOTTOM END ONLY
WITH SILICONE TUBING

BUOYANT PEACOCK QUILL
STEM OR COMMERCIAL
WAGGLER FLOAT

B

A, BB, AA OR
SWAN SHOT (SSG)
SET 3–4 IN FROM
HOOK

C

A

TENCH STANDS ON ITS
HEAD TO SUCK IN BAIT
FROM THE BOTTOM

SHOT IS DISLODGED AND
FLOAT RISES AS TENCH
RIGHTS ITSELF TO CHEW
BAIT
WHILE FLOAT RISES OR
'LIFTS', IT SUPPORTS THE
WEIGHT OF THE SHOT

WHEN TENCH KEEPS ITS HEAD
DOWN AND MOVES DIRECTLY
AWAY FROM THE ROD, THE
FLOAT DISAPPEARS
WITHOUT LIFTING

When numbers of tench are feeding in earnest and sending streams of bubbles up to the surface, the most effective method of presentation is to float-fish using the lift rig, and instantly hit any positive movement.

tench from the lakes at Wooton Underwood, the vast majority of anglers still get it wrong because they fail to grasp the basic principle of the lift. Once and for all let me explain how this great technique actually works.

The lift is particularly successful with, and suited to, the tench as a species because of the way in which they stand on their heads to suck in bottom-fished baits (see 'Feeding'). They are obliged to perform a headstand because their mouth is upturned. So when they decide that here on the bottom is a particle of food they fancy eating (your bait) they tilt their head down and suck it up. All being well they then return to an even keel while chewing the food. I have already mentioned that tench are equipped with powerful pharnygeal teeth to split a worm into pulp or crush the juices from maggots and casters. They then spit out the hook because it is indigestible – not necessarily as is often assumed, because it is something to be scared of – just as they do other unwanted items such as twigs, leaves, empty caddis cases, bits of weed, which get taken up as they vacuum the bottom. This is why an angler whose lift rig is incorrectly shotted (the shot being too far away from the hook) will reel in time and time again with empty maggot skins on the hook, without seeing the slightest indication of a bite.

The essence of fishing the lift is to set the float (a length of peacock quill or commercial waggler) a little overdepth,

attached bottom end only with a piece of silicone tubing and *not* locking shots. I'll say that again: *not* locking shots. You do not·want any shots anywhere near the float. All the shot loading, a BB, an AA, or a single swan shot (depending on casting requirements) must be fixed just 3–4 in from the hook (see fig. 12A). When the tench sucks up the bait and rights itself, thus dislodging the shot, the float starts to 'lift' (hence the method's name) and may even fall flat. But more importantly: while it is 'lifting' it is helping to support the weight of the shot. Of course, once the float lays completely flat (fig. 12B) the tench is fully supporting the weight of that shot and could eject the bait. This is why you should always strike as the float 'lifts'.

Some anglers suffer a mental block at this stage; because the float is still visible they do not consider the bite worth striking. If you leave the bite to develop further, the float may cock again and slowly slide beneath the surface in one of those classic 'Mr Crabtree' tench bites as the tench moves along the bottom directly away from the rod. However, this seldom happens. And you cannot risk waiting for such a positive indication because the tench will probably drop the bait.

This tench fisherman knows all about maximizing on bites when presenting the lift rig. He is holding the rod in a comfortable, relaxed, yet expectant manner, and is ready to strike quickly into the tiniest movement of the float tip.

If, however, from the moment it sucks up the bait the tench keeps its head down and carries on going directly away from the rod, the float without any pre-warning whatsoever (occasionally it might 'bob' first) will simply disappear as in fig. 12C. And this is the beauty behind the lift method – it allows you to interpret exactly what is happening down below.

When bites are expected at regular intervals you will convert considerably more (even the tiniest lifts and dips) into tench in the net if you hold the rod throughout. It may only take a split second to reach down and grab the rod set in rests, but the tench can blow the bait out even quicker. Besides, striking immediately allows you to bend the rod into a full curve and apply sufficient pressure against a tench hooked beside potential snags and to get it well under control before it can retaliate.

There is another advantage in holding the rod when fishing the lift. By gently moving the bait along the bottom you can encourage difficult tench to make a quick decision and grab the bait. This works especially well when the bait is presented over a clean bottom – either silt, mud or gravel – because as you slowly give the reel handle half a turn (providing the line is tight from float to rod tip) the inherent buoyancy of peacock quill will help the shot move along the bottom. Initially it will go under as you start to wind but will pop up again a second or two later. In the meantime, a tench may be aroused by the bait's sudden audacity in moving away, and make a sudden grab for it, resulting in a very quick 'lift' or 'dip'. If you are holding the rod you can strike these bites instantly, producing tench which would otherwise not be caught.

Tench can invariably be induced into feeding by bait movement, especially with baits which move anyway like maggots and worms. It is a characteristic trait which we all experience from time to time, the classic example being the ledger indicator which is yanked from your grasp (see 'Ledgering', p. 113) as you try desperately to reset it, having just moved the bait anything from a few inches to a couple of feet. And there is no better way of moving the bait while remaining ready to deal with an instant bite than presenting the lift rig.

For 'twitching' the bait over an uneven bottom, use a longer (and thus more buoyant) peacock quill than the shot

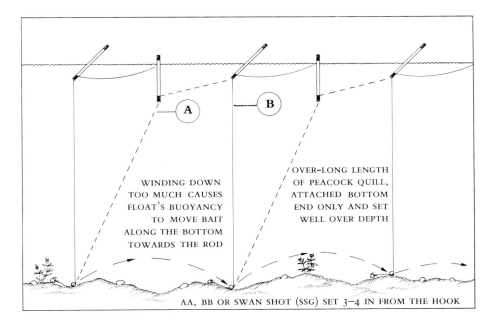

WINDING DOWN
TOO MUCH CAUSES
FLOAT'S BUOYANCY
TO MOVE BAIT
ALONG THE BOTTOM
TOWARDS THE ROD

OVER-LONG LENGTH
OF PEACOCK QUILL,
ATTACHED BOTTOM
END ONLY AND SET
WELL OVER DEPTH

AA, BB OR SWAN SHOT (SSG) SET 3–4 IN FROM THE HOOK

FIGURE 13 *Using the lift rig to twitch the bait along an uneven bottom*

requires. For example, if it is set shallower than the swim depth, the float should cock but with a good 2 in above the surface. Then reset it so that it is slightly over-depth and cast out, gently tightening up until only 1 in of the tip is visible (fig. 13A). You will know the set-up is correct when you wind down too much and the float lifts the shot along the bottom and keels over (fig. 13B). Just tighten up again, as this is exactly what it is supposed to do.

The lift can be used effectively with most baits (except large mouthfuls), and sometimes it pays to juggle about with the shot, moving it a little closer to the hook or a little further away than the recommended 3–4 in. When tench are especially shy in clear water conditions, I use a single BB (it is almost impossible to fish the lift effectively with a smaller shot) pinched on just 2 in from the hook and select a short, super-slim length of quill. Then I wind down until the top of the quill is a mere blimp in the surface film, and subsequently strike at the slightest movement up or down.

This super-sensitive rig is great for bugging the 'bubblers', tench which are rooting just beyond the marginal lilies quite close in, where the bubbles of individual fish can be identified. Make a calculated guess as to which direction the tench is heading and cast a little to the right or left of where bubbles last erupted. Be

There is nothing quite so nice as catching tench close in on light float tackle and a centre-pin reel.

FIGURE 14
(Opposite) *Bodied
waggler or driftbeater
rig*

impatient for bites, and keep casting to rising bubbles until an instant bite occurs. It is a fascinating and active way of taking tench.

Because an upward strike is imperative with the lift method to pick up the slack created by the tench lifting the bait and shot, it can only be used as a close-range technique. If you want to float-fish for tench which are actively feeding considerably further than say a couple of rod lengths out, particularly in windy weather, the line must be sunk or the float will drag under. This means you cannot strike upwards, or continue to use quite the same rig, so no longer can just a single shot be used.

Bodied waggler or driftbeater rig

To reach greater distances, you require a float taking a fair shotting capacity – anywhere from 3 AA to 2½ swan shot – and this means using a bodied waggler or a driftbeater. The float is locked by a BB on both sides, with the bulk shot set at mid depth, leaving a small shot (no. 1 or no. 3) to go near the hook, and a BB between it and the bulk shot (fig. 14).

To facilitate a quick change of float as surface conditions alter, use a swivel float attachment into which the float can instantly be pushed or removed. Lift bites on this rig are obviously not going to make the float come flying out of the water. However, with the bottom shot close to the hook, if the float is 'lifted' the float top will rise the same distance as it is sunk by that shot. So, after casting and winding the rig back over the swim with the rod tip beneath the surface to sink the line, memorize the level of the float in the water when the tip eventually settles once the BB shot is 'hanging', and then by how much further it sinks when the bottom shot hangs the bait just on the bottom.

In all probability most bites on this float rig will consist of a slow disappearance of the tip; you reply with a strong scything, sideways strike, keeping the rod tip low to the water to pick up maximum line and put the hook home. Gentle lift bites will occur, however, so watch carefully for the tip rising and always remember to strike sideways.

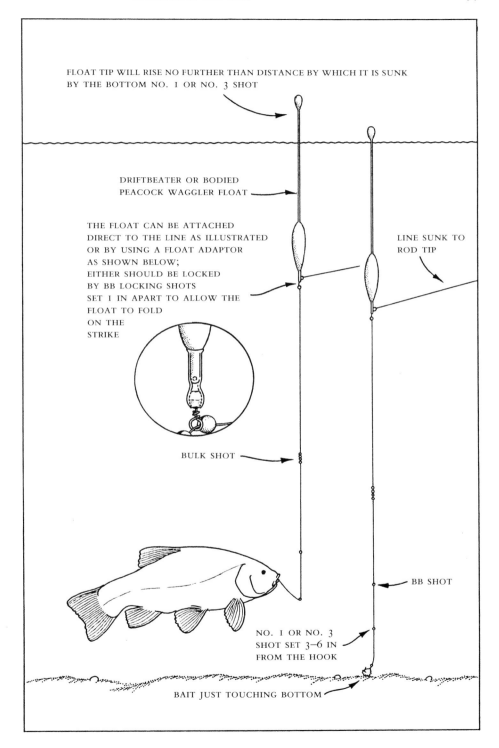

FLOAT TIP WILL RISE NO FURTHER THAN DISTANCE BY WHICH IT IS SUNK
BY THE BOTTOM NO. 1 OR NO. 3 SHOT

DRIFTBEATER OR BODIED
PEACOCK WAGGLER FLOAT

THE FLOAT CAN BE ATTACHED
DIRECT TO THE LINE AS ILLUSTRATED
OR BY USING A FLOAT ADAPTOR
AS SHOWN BELOW;
EITHER SHOULD BE LOCKED
BY BB LOCKING SHOTS
SET 1 APART TO ALLOW THE
FLOAT TO FOLD
ON THE
STRIKE

LINE SUNK TO
ROD TIP

BULK SHOT

BB SHOT

NO. 1 OR NO. 3
SHOT SET 3–6 IN
FROM THE HOOK

BAIT JUST TOUCHING BOTTOM

FIGURE 15
(Opposite) *Float
ledger rig*

Float ledger rig

When contemplating float-fishing for tench at distances beyond the casting potential of the previously mentioned lift, bodied waggler or driftbeater rigs, it makes sense to take all the shots off the line and put them on a mini ledger link stopped 10 in from the hook (fig. 15). With this float ledger rig, extremely long distances can be covered and the bait can be presented into areas where the ledgered bait is not practical, such as swims 40 yd out where a ledgered line cannot be sunk because of a large patch of lilies between the swim and the bank. The float ledger is also the best rig for presenting a static bait in extremely windy conditions, when either surface pull or underwater tow continually belly the line and submerge the tip of a delicately shotted float rig.

Having hooked it on a waggler float-ledger rig from just beyond the fringe of reeds hugging the lake edge, Terry Smith of Sheffield gives a big tench some wellie before bringing it to the net.

Strangely, in rough weather bites are invariably quite bold, and I can recall several outings when, even using three or four swan shots on the mini ledger, tench have moved them and actually given a lift bite. Most registrations, however, will consist of a positive sinking of the float tip, so ensure that enough of the tip is visible so that you can see this easily at distance – about 1½ in should do.

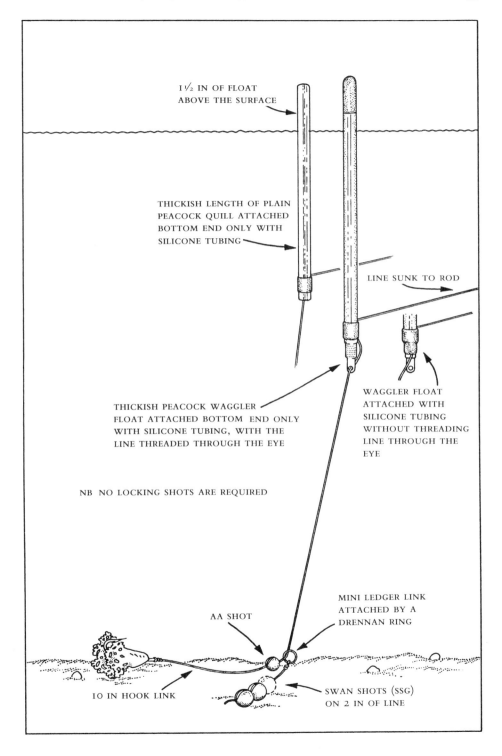

1½ IN OF FLOAT
ABOVE THE SURFACE

THICKISH LENGTH OF PLAIN
PEACOCK QUILL ATTACHED
BOTTOM END ONLY WITH
SILICONE TUBING

LINE SUNK TO ROD

THICKISH PEACOCK WAGGLER
FLOAT ATTACHED BOTTOM END ONLY
WITH SILICONE TUBING, WITH THE
LINE THREADED THROUGH THE EYE

WAGGLER FLOAT
ATTACHED WITH
SILICONE TUBING
WITHOUT THREADING
LINE THROUGH THE
EYE

NB NO LOCKING SHOTS ARE REQUIRED

MINI LEDGER LINK
ATTACHED BY A
DRENNAN RING

AA SHOT

10 IN HOOK LINK

SWAN SHOTS (SSG)
ON 2 IN OF LINE

FIGURE 16
(Opposite) *Zoomer
rig*

I like a long, thickish, straight peacock waggler for float ledgering, and attach it to the line with a ⅜ in length of silicone tubing around the bottom stem.

The zoomer rig

This is a deadly float rig for placing the bait close up to reed-lines or against lily-beds in clear water conditions, where bites materialize only if the bait is presented in the tench's habitat (fig. 16A). Simply rig up an onion or zoomer with the bulk shot at the base of the float. After plummeting the depth accurately, pinch on a BB shot around 5 in from the hook, so it comes to rest just on the bottom. Then, because the float precedes the hook and shot, you can allow it almost to bump against the reed-line before stopping the cast, knowing the bait will angle back down through the water to settle mere inches away from the leading reeds, in full view of patrolling tench.

This method also pays dividends on even-depth, clear-watered lakes and meres where dinghies or punts are used (fig. 16B). If beds of marginal reeds, rushes or sedges are the only cover, that is where the tench will be. Row up quietly to within practical casting distance and position the boat side-on to the reed-line. Anchor it by slipping a mud-weight over the side at each end.

As the float cannot be wound back with the rod tip held beneath the surface to sink the line (which would only bring the bait away from the reeds), take along a small (medicine) bottle of neat washing-up liquid and dab a finger-full over the spool every so often. The line will then sink willingly and instantly, after which you can very gently tighten up without pulling the float away from the reeds. Hold the rod whenever bites are expected.

Keep catapulting fragments of loose feed like sweetcorn, maggots, casters or worms along the reed-line for a distance of several yards either side of the float, and tench might be encouraged to work the area all day long.

As a last resort when bites appear to have finally dried up once the sun rises high in the sky, try this favourite old all-or-nothing ruse. Row over to reeds and with an oar spend 15 minutes clouding up the bottom silt. Then return to your anchorage and commence fishing.

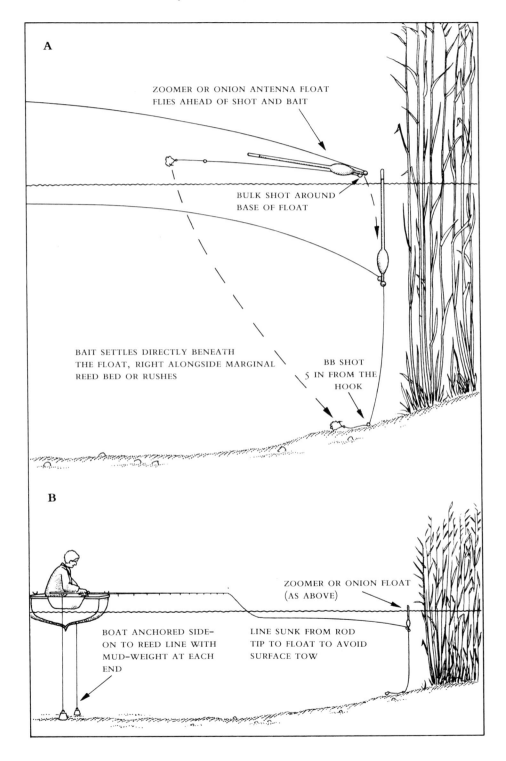

A

ZOOMER OR ONION ANTENNA FLOAT
FLIES AHEAD OF SHOT AND BAIT

BULK SHOT AROUND
BASE OF FLOAT

BAIT SETTLES DIRECTLY BENEATH
THE FLOAT, RIGHT ALONGSIDE MARGINAL
REED BED OR RUSHES

BB SHOT
5 IN FROM THE
HOOK

B

ZOOMER OR ONION FLOAT
(AS ABOVE)

BOAT ANCHORED SIDE-
ON TO REED LINE WITH
MUD-WEIGHT AT EACH
END

LINE SUNK FROM ROD
TIP TO FLOAT TO AVOID
SURFACE TOW

Anchoring the boat quietly away from the reed beds, and casting a zoomer float rig close up alongside the stems, puts the bait exactly where tench feed naturally.

The flat peacock rig

When tackling dense reed-lines along your own bank, either from wooden staging or from marshy ground, it is a waste of time to cast out over the reeds and expect tench to feed in open water, unless the water is well coloured. They are much more likely to be mere feet away, working through the reeds or rushes (see 'Feeding').

Such swims demand a stealthy approach (fig. 17). You need to sit or kneel a few feet back from the water-line with a bait hanging right beneath the rod tip just 2 to 3 yd out, where tench will be feeding between the stems. The type of float is not really important at such close range. A tiny waggler, or even 2 in of slim unpainted peacock quill, will suffice. In the absence of wind or surface tow, I like the quill fixed top and bottom to present it lying 'flat' on the surface.

The beauty of the 'flat' float is that unbelievably confident bites will result. The quill slides along the surface, following the direction of the tench, and disappears with the same confidence fish show to freelined offerings. Only one small shot is attached, around 12 in from the bait. It does not matter what size shot you use, because it doesn't cock the float. If you are fishing right in amongst marginal stems pre-baiting is not really necessary because the tench are already there. More often than not, groups of

As far as the hungry tench is concerned, this weedy corner of the lake is ideal. Free-lining, or use of the flat peacock float rig with the hook tied direct to a 6 lb reel line and baits like a whole lobworm or luncheon meat cube, are recommended tactics.

stems can be seen swaying as fish root between them. However, you will need to creep about to catch them at such close quarters. Just scatter a handful of bait fragments among the stems (pieces of flake or broken worms) to keep fish in the area, and to encourage them to return each time one is caught and they temporarily disappear.

FIGURE 17 *Flat peacock rig. The peacock quill is fixed top and bottom. The hook bait can be bread flake, lobworm, etc.*

KNEEL OR SIT WELL BACK FROM THE WATERSIDE —
TO CAPITALISE ON TENCH THAT MAY BE WORKING
IN AMONGST REED OR RUSH BEDS

2″ PEACOCK
QUILL FIXED

SMALL SHOT

Though the float may be light, this is certainly not a light-tackle method. You will need all of a 6 lb test line to subdue even modest-sized tench of 2–3 lb in exciting hit and haul tussles.

FLOAT FISHING AT NIGHT

Without question, and especially where the water is gin-clear for most of the summer, fishing for tench from dusk into darkness, perhaps even all night through, offers the best chance of success. I know several lakes, meres and pits where, for the last two hours of daylight, you need to scale down almost to match tackle to encourage even an occasional, tentative bite. As soon as the light starts to go, however, and it becomes difficult for the human eye to distinguish the bottom through just 2 to 3 ft of clear water, the tench lose their natural caution and start to bite positively. And this phenomenon is not applicable only to hard-fished, public tench fisheries.

So if bites are hard to come by wherever you fish during the daytime, try a spot of night fishing. It can be magical, provided you choose a suitable night on your first attempt. Tench are not likely to be receptive to your bait, for instance, during a howling gale accompanied by torrential rain and a sudden drop in temperature.

If you prefer the simplicity of float fishing and there is a reasonable depth along the margins where tench can be encouraged to feed with a little pre-baiting, the good old lift method is the rig to use (p. 88). Follow exactly my advice for presenting the lift, and fix a luminous element to the top of the float.

Whether your session turns into an all-nighter, or lasts for just a few hours, you want to avoid eye strain, and the most pleasant of luminous elements to watch continuously are the chemical 'starlights', which come in a choice of three sizes. These consist of a clear plastic tube containing two chemicals which, once you bend the tube and shake it, mix together and become luminous for about eight hours. I prefer the mini 'starlights', which come two to a packet complete with a length of clear tubing. If you are using a thin stem of peacock quill, the tubing supplied fits snuggly over the tip with the starlight slotting into the other end.

Both the Drennan polywag and onion floats (which both work well fished lift style), of any shotting capacity, also have tips of the right diameter. Alternatively, purchase the Drennan clear-bodied, insert-crystal wagglers, which have detachable tips into which the Drennan 'night light' can be fitted. These are available in three sizes, large (for distance fishing), standard and minis, the last two being quite sufficient and easily seen just like the 'starlights', up to three rod lengths out.

As bites at night tend to be far more positive than those experienced in the daytime, resist the temptation to wind the float tip down so only the merest tip is visible, or you will be forever striking at ghosts. By all means hold the rod to capitalize on bites when they are occurring frequently, but when times are slow, try to relax by positioning the rod close to hand, supported horizontally on two rests.

Wherever there is a slight draw on the surface, the float might be slowly dragged under. Simply push the back rod rest down a little to angle the tip of the rod upwards, thus lifting sufficient line off the surface for the float tip to reappear. You will gradually learn these little tricks. You will also quickly discover to switch on a torch *only* when it is absolutely necessary (such as when the line is tangled) because night vision is instantly ruined by torchlight. It takes several minutes before your eyes can readjust to the dark again, making items such as the bait and your landing-net visible once more.

LEDGERING

Although there are dozens of different float rigs for catching tench (and everyone has his favourites), the selection just described should prove more than adequate wherever and whenever you fish. There will, however, be many occasions throughout the summer months when the pleasure of watching a float must reluctantly be replaced by the effectiveness of the ledger (and particularly of feeder fishing) if you wish to catch tench from a wide spectrum of waters.

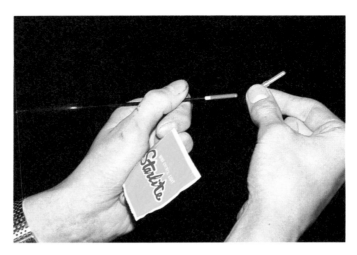

Tench inhabiting distant troughs and gullies situated, say, 40 yd or more out from the bank in huge gravel pit complexes can only be tackled effectively by ledgering. Large, clear-watered estate lakes where the tench always seem to keep well out because the marginal water is so shallow, or because there is a complete absence of soft weed, again demand ledgering tactics. So too do waters with hard bottoms, such as brick-laid reservoirs and deep, newly dug gravel or clay pits, where weed beds or layers of silt have yet to accumulate, and where subsequently the tench may never be seen bubbling enough to pinpoint them with float tackle. Ledgering at least gives you the option of searching for them 'grid style' until bites materialize.

In fact, most large sheets of water are far more effectively fished with ledgering techniques because of weather conditions alone. To cast accurately and control a float over long distances in the windy conditions which invariably prevail on open sheets of water is an impossible task. And on the calmest day, there might well be a draw or pull on the surface to irritate the most ardent of float-fishermen.

Fixed paternoster

The fixed paternoster is a simple follow-on from freelining (p. 85), and is used to reach fish beyond the casting range

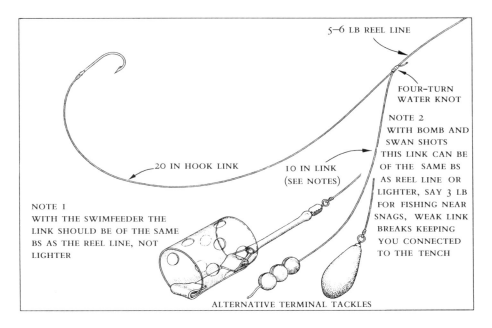

5–6 LB REEL LINE

FOUR–TURN
WATER KNOT

NOTE 2
WITH BOMB AND
SWAN SHOTS
THIS LINK CAN BE
OF THE SAME BS
AS REEL LINE OR
LIGHTER, SAY 3 LB
FOR FISHING NEAR
SNAGS, WEAK LINK
BREAKS KEEPING
YOU CONNECTED
TO THE TENCH

20 IN HOOK LINK

10 IN LINK
(SEE NOTES)

NOTE 1
WITH THE SWIMFEEDER THE
LINK SHOULD BE OF THE SAME
BS AS THE REEL LINE, NOT
LIGHTER

ALTERNATIVE TERMINAL TACKLES

of weightless tackle. It is formed by adding a simple fixed-bomb paternoster to the reel line 20 in above the hook (fig. 18). The fixed-bomb paternoster comprises a 10 in link (of reel line), tied in using a four-turn water knot (p. 53), to which a bomb or a string of swan shots is added. Because their weight is distributed over a greater surface area, a string of swan shots (unlike a dense bomb), does not drop down through thick weed. Instead, the swan shot usually rest on top. And provided they have been pinched on lightly, they will slide off easily even if they become snagged. Conversely, if snags are expected, use a lighter test for the link, say 3 lb, which should break and ditch the swan shots or bomb, leaving you free to play the tench. Incidentally, I rarely use less than a 5 lb test reel line when ledgering for tench; more often than not I put my faith in 6 lb test, which copes with the rigours of continuous casting and being dragged across weed-beds, over shallow bars and even along the bottom. You can use lighter hook lengths, but there is no point in going lighter on the reel line. To present a buoyant bait, like an air injected lob, bread crust or a pop-up boilie, several inches above dense bottom weed simply add a swan shot or two a few inches above the hook (fig. 19).

This simple ledger rig will suffice for a whole variety of

FIGURE 18 *Fixed paternoster ledger*

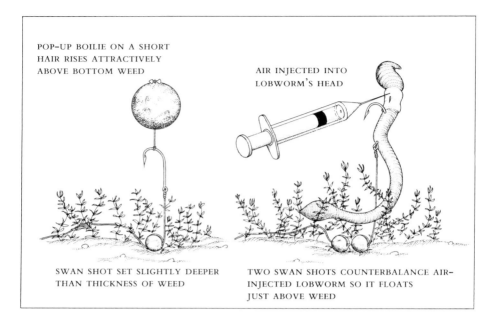

POP-UP BOILIE ON A SHORT
HAIR RISES ATTRACTIVELY
ABOVE BOTTOM WEED

AIR INJECTED INTO
LOBWORM'S HEAD

SWAN SHOT SET SLIGHTLY DEEPER
THAN THICKNESS OF WEED

TWO SWAN SHOTS COUNTERBALANCE AIR-
INJECTED LOBWORM SO IT FLOATS
JUST ABOVE WEED

FIGURE 19 *Presenting buoyant baits over dense bottom weed*

baits in addition to boilies and worms, including meat cubes, sweetcorn, maggots, soft pastes and bread flake, presented wherever loose feed or groundbait has been either catapulted or thrown in. Beyond this range you simply exchange the bomb or swan shots for a swimfeeder – to be more precise, an open-ended swimfeeder.

Feeder fishing

If conditions require a slow dispersal of, say, maggots, such as when ledgering for tench during the winter in very mild spells (see 'Winter tench', pp. 41–3), a block-end feeder such as the Drennan 'feeder link' fits the bill perfectly. However, in summer this is not the case. Then I want the feeder to explode its load just before, or as, it hits bottom, thus creating an instant food source for the tench to home in on. The best open-ended feeders are the plain, plastic, clear or green open-ends with a lead strip at the base, or the self-weighted cage feeders. Both permit the instant bait dispersal of breadcrumb groundbait, provided that the crumbs are not over-wetted. Coarse, slightly dampened crumb is preferable, because it really does explode once the crumbs expand on impact with the water.

For putting out just groundbait, I use both cage and plastic open-ended feeders. If I want a crumb plug at each end, with a filling of hook bait samples like corn, maggots or casters, the open-ended feeder is best. Incidentally, to stop feeder maggots from burrowing into soft silt and disappearing (something they can do with surprising speed) immerse them for just a couple of seconds in boiling water and dry off with maize meal or bread crumbs. They will look a little 'stretched' when killed in this manner, but tench gobble them up just the same and I cannot remember suffering any lack of bites when using them on the hook.

Do not worry about the heavy splash made by a feeder when it hits the water, because the tench come to associate it with the arrival of free food. The secret is to keep casting the feeder out every 10 minutes or so, whether tench respond or not. In this way, small piles of bait are deposited over a fairly tight area, ready for the moment when they move in to inspect it. And they will – just have faith in their inquisitiveness.

In effect, you create (often in a ridiculously short space of time) your own tench swim, with fish eventually moving about on the bottom from one pile of bait to another. Casting needs to be accurate so that you do not spread bait, and therefore tench, over too wide an area.

A two-rod set-up is beneficial when feeder-fishing. Double the bait is deposited, and you have the option at will to use one of the rods as the 'locator' when you think the tench may have moved position, keeping the other over the original baited area.

Striking

The ideal tool for ledgering, with or without feeders, is a 1¼ lb text curve, 11 ft or 12 ft carbon Avon rod (see p. 46–8). I prefer the 12-footer for optimum line pick up when long-range fishing. After casting out, each rod is pointed at the bait to minimize resistance from biting fish and to maximize striking efficiency. Remember that in really shallow water a low, sideways strike will pick up more line because it pulls it through the water as opposed to lifting it upwards against the surface tension (fig. 20A). On the other hand, when presenting the bait into deep-

Ledgering into deep gullies way out from the margins in really clear-watered gravel pits is the most effective way of catching tench right through the day. A reduction in both hook-length strength and hook sizes is imperative for inducing bites in bright conditions.

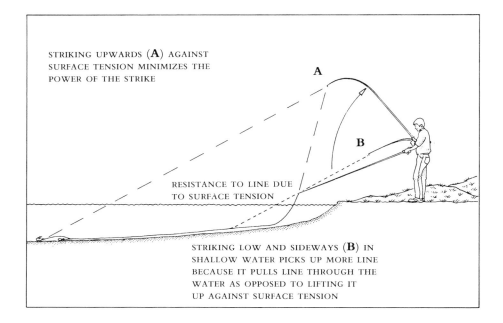

STRIKING UPWARDS (**A**) AGAINST
SURFACE TENSION MINIMIZES THE
POWER OF THE STRIKE

A

B

RESISTANCE TO LINE DUE
TO SURFACE TENSION

STRIKING LOW AND SIDEWAYS (**B**) IN
SHALLOW WATER PICKS UP MORE LINE
BECAUSE IT PULLS LINE THROUGH THE
WATER AS OPPOSED TO LIFTING IT
UP AGAINST SURFACE TENSION

FIGURE 20A
*Striking in
shallow water*

water swims, an upwards strike is more advantageous
(fig. 20B).

Try to tighten up gently after casting, to sink the line
fully, so that it settles in a straight line between feeder and
rod tip, not in a huge belly. Then clip on the indicator (see
pp. 55–60). A little washing-up liquid dabbed around the
line on the spool will help it sink quickly, so keep a bottle
handy. In strong winds, endeavour to fish directly into the
wind. Otherwise, pinch a swan shot or two on to the
bobbin line to stop any underwater tow bellying the line
between feeder and rod tip, thus reducing the effectiveness
of the strike. Remember that if the line is not reasonably
tight from feeder to rod, setting the hook becomes more of
a problem the further out you fish. This may occur when
you are fishing over dense beds of soft weed if the rods are
set too low to the surface. Bite indication will be hampered
if the line actually rests on the weed, resulting in a much
reduced movement of the bobbin. The remedy here is to
set the rods as high as you can, keeping as much line as
possible off the weed and keeping it relatively tight from
tip to feeder. Unfortunately this becomes difficult in
strong winds because extra line above the surface creates
additional wind resistance. The only recourse is to add still
more swan shots to the bobbin retaining-cord.

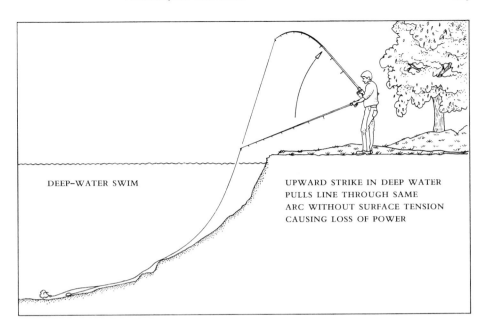

DEEP–WATER SWIM

UPWARD STRIKE IN DEEP WATER
PULLS LINE THROUGH SAME
ARC WITHOUT SURFACE TENSION
CAUSING LOSS OF POWER

Bite indication

FIGURE 20B
*Striking in
deep water*

During the initial hours of feeder-fishing in a 'new' swim, bites will invariably consist of really positive lifts of the bobbin, with the Optonic screeching out several bleeps before the bobbin clangs against the butt ring. In this situation, allow a drop of around 18 in. The choice of combining the bobbin with an electric alarm as the front rod rest is, of course, optional. I would suggest, however, that where long all-day or all-night sessions are concerned, the excessive concentration demanded by staring contin-ually at the bobbins, not daring to look away in case one moves (and that is when they always do move) is reason enough to use the combination. In addition, the alarm/ bobbin set up is by far the most efficient for all feeder-fishing for tench. I find that it allows a very relaxed approach to fishing, giving me time to study wildlife through the binoculars and to scan the surface for bubbles. Yet I am ready to strike instantly the very second the alarm issues its warning bleeps.

Bonus fish can often be caught as a result of studying surface activity in between bites. Tench caught well away from the main feeding area often result from quickly

John dares the bobbin to move and stands poised for a long sweeping strike when distance fishing the feeder for tench in a shallow, Norfolk estate lake. Twitcher-hitting at its best.

reeling in one of the baits and repositioning it close to any sudden eruption of bubbles, or to a porpoising fish.

The twitching cycle

As the tench become more preoccupied with loose feed deposited by the feeder, and as your casting becomes more accurate, concentrating good numbers of tench into a comparatively confined area, tiny twitch bites – 1 to 2 in lifts or drops of the bobbin – will become commonplace.

Now is the time to reduce both the bobbin drop so that small movements are more noticeable, and the hook length to just 6 in enabling you to see bites much earlier. Keep the 10 in feeder link (fig. 21). Quite simply the tench are no longer moving away with the bait to another patch of food, they are consuming it on the spot. Bites which merely lift or drop back the bobbin by ¼ in may seem to be the work of small fish instead of tench, but that is because they have become so preoccupied and so confident, with an excess of food spread around them, that they have little reason to move.

If on a standard hook tail (18–20 in long) you repeatedly reel in sucked maggots or sweetcorn skins, or your worms have had all the goodness crushed out of them, the bait must have been sucked back to the pharnygeal teeth, chewed for a while, and then spat out. It is wise to strike promptly at the slightest twitch or jingle of the bobbin once the twitching cycle begins – once you have shortened the hook length.

On calm days you can forget the bobbin altogether after tightening up, and simply watch the line itself where it enters the water, hitting the slightest lift or drop back no matter how seemingly insignificant.

If bites still prove conspicuous by their absence, and you believe tench are still in the swim – as may be the case in the middle of the day when parts of the terminal rig look far more obvious in very clear water – it is time to reduce the hook length from 6, 5 or 4 lb to just 3 lb, and to step down in hook size, presenting smaller baits. While a number 10 hook holding four grains of corn or five maggots may be the taking formula at 6 am, by 11.30 am, when the sun is high above the water, those same tench

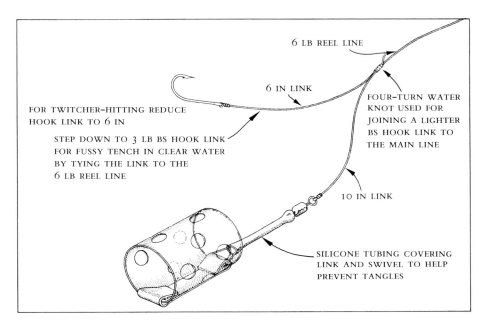

6 LB REEL LINE

6 IN LINK

FOR TWITCHER–HITTING REDUCE
HOOK LINK TO 6 IN

FOUR–TURN WATER
KNOT USED FOR
JOINING A LIGHTER
BS HOOK LINK TO
THE MAIN LINE

STEP DOWN TO 3 LB BS HOOK LINK
FOR FUSSY TENCH IN CLEAR WATER
BY TYING THE LINK TO THE
6 LB REEL LINE

10 IN LINK

SILICONE TUBING COVERING
LINK AND SWIVEL TO HELP
PREVENT TANGLES

FIGURE 21
'Twitcher-hitting'

may not provide you with a hittable bite until you offer them a size 16 holding two casters. When bites are not forthcoming, it is worth trying anything. However, don't be tempted to go down to a lighter hook length than the tench can be safely extracted with. Consider the weed growth, snags, and the general size of the fish expected and only step down accordingly.

I like to try to stimulate bites by constantly changing hook baits (regardless of what has been fed in), from maggots to corn, flake to worms and back again. Occasionally a buoyant bait presented on the drop will bring immediate action simply because it's different. Or try offerings like casters and crust cocktails, casters and corn, flake and maggots, and so on. Never be afraid to experiment. Try twitching the bait in, pausing for 30 seconds or so between each half or full slow crank of the handle. This of course is suicidal in thick weed, but where the bottom is reasonably clean it is a deadly technique which often leaves you next to no time between twitches to reset the bobbin before it is yanked upwards.

As you might a float, try and relate movements of the bobbin to what is actually happening at the end of your feeder rig. For instance, wherever the bobbin jerks upwards a couple of inches and then suddenly falls

During the brightness and heat of midday, tench can still be en-encouraged to bite even in clear water. Small hooks and the ability to hit the tiniest of twitches are the pre-requisites for consist-ent result.

A small male tench taken feeder-fishing on light tackle in bright conditions.

completely slack in a glorious drop back, this is not the fish first moving away and then turning around and swimming back towards the rod, as you might be forgiven for thinking. It is the ledger rig tightening (as the bobbin jerks up) immediately before the tension reaches too much and the feeder is pulled towards the rod, whereupon the bobbin suddenly drops. The tench has in fact been moving towards the rod from the moment it picked up the bait. These are always definite bites, because the tench is not

going to let go, and a long sweeping strike to mend the
loose line nearly always connects.

*Enjoying a bout of
'twitcher hitting',
John becomes
cavalierish and pre-
pares to hand out a
tench instead of reach-
ing for the net.*

Bolt-rig fishing

Moving away from feeder fishing we finally come to the
shock or bolt rig. This was first devised for carp fishing,
but also works well for wary tench. It is especially useful
when fishing for tench which share carp fisheries, and
which have been weaned on to carp baits, namely boilies
and hard particles such as peanuts and black-eyed beans.

As can be seen from fig. 22, a rotten bottom is used on
the bomb link, tied on to the main line with a four-turn
water knot. If it snags up in weed you can continue to play

the tench, losing only a 1½ oz bomb. Reel line is 6 lb (unless big tench are anticipated, in which case step up to 8 lb straight through) to a size 10 or 8 hook. If you always sit next to the rods (within grabbing distance) this method works best fished with a closed bale arm, although some may consider this rather risky. After casting and dunking the rod tip to lower the line along the bottom contours, support the rod in two rests, pointing it at the bait. Leave a slight bow between surface and rod tip before clipping on a bobbin or monkey climber half way between butt ring and reel, hanging on a 12 in drop. This scaled-down fixed-lead rig then catches tench in the same way as it does a carp which happens along and sucks in the boilie or particle.

As the bait is gulped back to the pharnygeal teeth for chewing, the tench suddenly (provided the hook and bomb links are not too long) feels the lead. It then quickly shuts its mouth and does a runner, forgetting the bait it was about to chew. Meanwhile, the hook is pulled down to the lips and jerked in by the fixed lead. When the line tightens a second later, with the tench 2 or 3 ft away and gaining speed, the hook is really banged home. While all this is happening (in a split second or so), the Optonic screeches a multiple bleep, followed by the rod trying to leave the rod rests. However, if the butt ring is jammed up against the Optonic, the rod will stay in place. You are then, without even having to strike, suddenly into a tench.

The bait may be side-hooked, or, if the tench are particularly wary, sleeved on to a fine (¾ lb) hair just ½ in long. Invariably a single bait produces a better hooking ratio to bites, while a mini-string of tiny boilies may induce more offers. Once the hook baits are positioned loose feed, and an additional attractor such as hempseed, can be scattered around with a catapult.

Good tenching

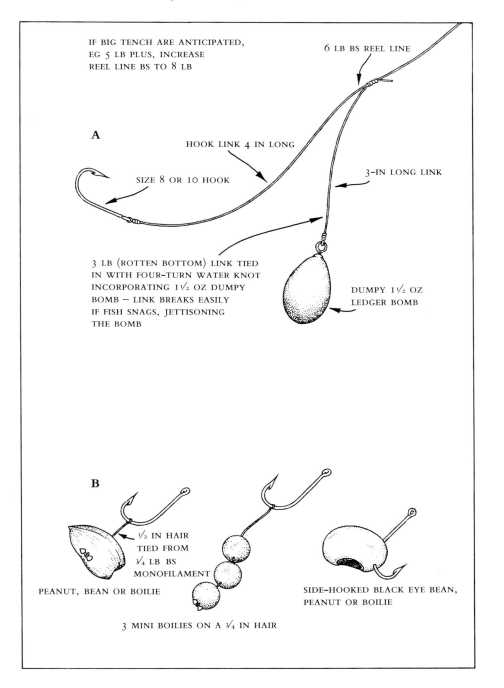

IF BIG TENCH ARE ANTICIPATED,
EG 5 LB PLUS, INCREASE
REEL LINE BS TO 8 LB

6 LB BS REEL LINE

A

HOOK LINK 4 IN LONG

3-IN LONG LINK

SIZE 8 OR 10 HOOK

3 LB (ROTTEN BOTTOM) LINK TIED
IN WITH FOUR-TURN WATER KNOT
INCORPORATING 1½ OZ DUMPY
BOMB — LINK BREAKS EASILY
IF FISH SNAGS, JETTISONING
THE BOMB

DUMPY 1½ OZ
LEDGER BOMB

B

½ IN HAIR
TIED FROM
¾ LB BS
MONOFILAMENT

PEANUT, BEAN OR BOILIE

SIDE-HOOKED BLACK EYE BEAN,
PEANUT OR BOILIE

3 MINI BOILIES ON A ¾ IN HAIR

Waiting for his free-lined whole swan mussel bait to be sucked up from beside the roots of a dense bed of white lilies, the tench fisherman has time to reflect.

INDEX